Welcome! You woke up recently and something was different. It's like someone else was looking out of your eyes at you in the mirror. You can't shake the feeling of dissatisfaction with certain aspects of your life, and the even greater feeling that there is something significant that you don't know.

If you are holding this book, it is because the river of your life has brought it to you. Chance is a powerful thing. If you are currently questioning life, facing a challenge or simply curious about your own humanity, you are in the right place. Read on. May this roadmap help you find what you seek.

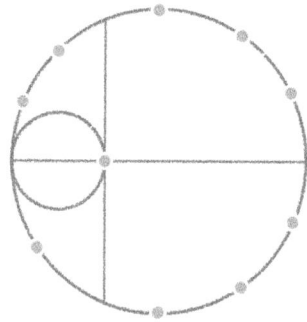

Purna Asatti

A roadmap to self understanding through complete connection

Amy Kathryn Colleen Messegee, PhD

Trend Factor Press

Trend Factor Press, a division of Sparticle Concepts LLC
1530 P B Lane #M4819, Wichita Falls, TX 76302-2612
KathrynColleen.com

Copyright © 2019-2021 by Amy Kathryn Colleen Messegee, PhD. All rights reserved.

This content is protected by United States and International copyright laws. No part of this content may be reproduced or distributed without the written consent of the author.

ISBN-13 978-1-7356943-6-8
(Paperback, English)

This book has an accompanying music album, podcast, multiple translations, and many extra resources. To contact the author, or to find more information about this book, translations, other publications, podcasts and music, please visit KathrynColleen.com. Your thoughts and questions are welcomed.

Guide

Where This Roadmap Came From	8
How To Use This Book	9
Resources	10

Your Destination Is Unique.... The Road To Get There Is NOT — 15

- What You Get When You Put It All Together - The Cycle Of Human Development — 18
- The Key To Your Journey - CONNECTION — 21
- The Symbol - Something To Help You Focus On Connection — 22
- A Private Journey — 24
- Before You Begin - Physical, Mental And Financial Safety — 26
- Let's Go! — 27

Stage One: Everything Is Me — 29

- Grounding Yourself - Connecting To Your Time, Attention And Spaces — 36
- Forms Of Meditation And Prayer — 41
- Connecting To The Emotional Roots Of Your Choices — 44
- Trusting Yourself — 45
- Trusting Your River / Universe / The Divine — 46

Stage Two: I Am Everything Except Experiences And Reflexes — 49

- Connecting To Experiences — 56
- Connecting To Your Needs — 58
- Connecting To Your Body - Sleep, Regeneration And Movement — 60
- Manifesting - A Comprehensive And Simple Guide — 62
- Manifesting Struggle - Swimming Against Your River — 64

Stage Three: I Am My Needs | 67

    Connecting To Your Sexuality - Mind, Body And Energy | 74

    Connecting To Yourself - You Are More Than Your Needs And Wants | 76

    Connecting To Others - Seeing Their Humanity Through Their Needs | 78

    Connecting To Your Internal Energy And Feelings | 79

    Connecting To Your Money - Getting Out Of Debt | 82

Stage Four: Others Have Needs Too | 85

    Connecting To Yourself And Others - Attending To Needs As Part Of A Regular Routine | 92

    Connecting To Yourself - Recognizing And Removing Negative Patterns | 94

    Connecting To Your Ideology - Define Your Ideology And Put It Into Practice | 96

    Connecting To Your Money - Solidifying Your Savings Engine | 98

Stage Five: I Am My Value Set / Ideology / Religion / Beliefs | 101

    Connecting To Yourself - Reading About Other Ideologies And Updating Your Own | 108

    Connecting To Others - Seeing Their Humanity Through Their Ideology | 110

Stage Six: To Each Their Own | 115

    Connecting To Yourself - Taking Responsibility For Your Life | 123

    Connecting To Your Body - Setting Goals And Making Progress | 124

    Connecting To Yourself - Forgiving And Accepting Yourself As Human | 126

    Connecting To Your Heart - Breaking The Trance Of Unworthiness | 128

    Connecting To Others - Seeing Yourself In Others | 130

    Connecting To Others - Forgiving And Accepting Others As Human | 132

Stage Seven: Questioning Everything — 135

    Connecting To Your Faith Through Questioning — 144

    Connecting To Doubt - Questioning Everything — 146

    Connecting To Yourself - Healing Your Scars — 148

    Connecting To Yourself - Identifying And Replacing Limiting Beliefs — 150

    Connecting To The Infinit Silence / Divine — 152

Stage Eight: I Am A Child Of The Universe / Divine — 155

    Connecting To Universal Truths — 162

    Connecting To The Universe / Divine - Letting Go Of Knowing — 164

    Connecting To The Silent Observer — 166

    Connecting To Your Purpose - Methods For Finding It — 168

    Connecting To Your Reality - Designing Your Future — 170

    Connecting To Others - Seeing Their Truth — 171

Stage Nine: I Am A Consciousness Trapped In This Body — 173

    Connecting To This Moment - Presence, Mindfulness And Intuition — 180

    Connecting Completely To Your Partner — 182

    Connecting To The One Consciousness — 184

    The Big Bang And The One Consciousness (A Thought Experiment) — 186

    Connecting To Your Intellect - Building Skills For Your Purpose — 190

Stage Ten: I Am The ONE Consciousness — 193

    Connecting To Higher Wisdom - Beyond Intuition — 200

    Connecting To The Oneness And Your Influence — 202

    Staying Connected - Recognizing Separation Triggers — 204

Stage Eleven: I Am The One Consciousness And The Physical Manifestation Simultaneously And There Is No Difference   207

    Connecting To Your Reality - $E = mc^2$ 216

    Maintaining It All   218

    Seeking Complete Connection   220

Accelerating Your Development   223

    Mentors, Teachers, Guides And Coaches   224

    Reiki And The Role Of Energy Work   226

    Questions, Answers And Additional Resources   229

Big List Of Great Questions   231

Notes And Revelations   238

Where This Roadmap Came From

I was 31 when I woke up. I remember it vividly. I looked in the mirror like I had been asleep in the car and someone else had driven us into a ditch. I did not like where things were going physically or financially, or career-wise and I felt like there was something really important that I was completely clueless about. I wanted to take the journey that so many others had taken - the journey of self-development and self-understanding towards a more fulfilling life. This journey has taken more than a decade of walking through some of the worst and best times in my life. What I wish I had back then, was a roadmap. I wish I had something to guide me on what to do first, and what to do next, and the next step after that, etc. If I had been handed a roadmap to self-development back then, I might have gotten to this point a LOT sooner and with a lot less pain. Perhaps twelve years could have been more like one or two and many mistakes and wasted effort could have been avoided. If I had a roadmap, I might have been able to get quickly to my purpose, and a life of peace and joy. So **this roadmap is for you**. May it guide you on your journey and speed you to where you want to be, wherever that is.

This roadmap is the result of aggregating the research and writings of more than fifty scholars, researchers, authors, speakers, and thought leaders over that twelve year period. It stands on the shoulders of giants to distill their findings and influence into a single coherent roadmap that accelerates your self-understanding. It is a process and a practice for keeping you in the beautiful states of your choosing through complete connection to yourself and every aspect of your life.

> *"If I had been handed a roadmap back then, I might have gotten to this point a LOT sooner and with a lot less pain."*

How To Use This Book

This book is a roadmap for self-understanding through complete connection. It guides you through eleven stages, each with tasks, recommended resources and questions to spark your thinking. Work through each task starting from Stage One. When you complete the roadmap, you can read parts of it again and repeat exercises to help keep you in the stages you want experience most.

Although it is simple, it may not be easy... This journey will not be instant. Depending on where you are now, you may have significant baggage to unpack and you may have major mistakes to correct. Your circle of friends and family may change dramatically. If you are with the wrong person, you are about to find out. If you are in the wrong career, that too is about to become clear. That dissatisfaction you feel is based in your soul and to feel the kind of peace that you seek, you will need to face the realities of your past choices and start consciously making better ones.

If you are lucky, perhaps you are not too far off the mark. But even if you are with the right person and in the right career, this journey is not easy. You will face yourself - your beautiful reality and your dark side. Your humanity will be laid bare for you to see and you will be challenged to love yourself, not in spite of your humanity, but because of it. **On the other side of this journey is a life so amazing and joyous; peaceful and content, that words will fail and all you will feel is gratitude for each day.**

If you currently enjoy a particular religion, you can use this process to develop a deeper level of faith. However, the path to get there includes questioning everything and growing to see your deity in a higher, more expanded role and from a less anthropomorphic perspective. Ultimately, you will come to recognize the immensity of your deity's reach and what they have gifted you.

Work through each task starting from Stage One. When you complete the roadmap, you can read parts of it again and repeat exercises to help keep you in the stages you want experience most.

Please think long and hard about whether you are ready. If you choose to proceed, you alone are responsible for what happens; good, bad, wonderful, ecstatic, amazing, terrifying, and all.

If and when you are ready, read on.

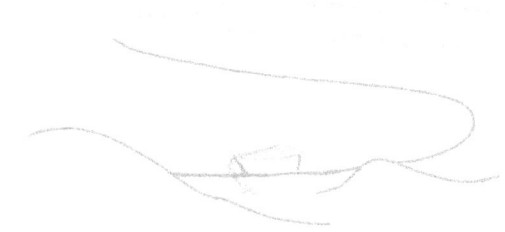

Resources

The following authors' work directly inspired or influenced this roadmap. They are listed in no particular order along with a quick note on what I learned from them. No one is more important or profound than another. Consider them important resources for your journey. Seek them out and let their writings, podcasts and other works influence you and contribute to your connections. You will see some of their specific writings and podcasts mentioned in the roadmap in each stage. Throughout your journey, you should seek as many resources from these and other authors as you are compelled to find. Let your natural curiosity lead you to the right inspiration at the right time.

Seek as many resources from these and other authors as you are compelled to find.

- Tara Brach (meditation, mindfulness, connecting to your body and reality)

- Tim Ferriss (rejecting and replacing societal rules, defining your ideal life and achieving it, questioning everything, 80/20 analysis, connecting to your body, learning languages and other skills quickly)

- Dr. Henry Cloud and Dr. John Townsend (setting healthy boundaries on your time, attention and space)

- Dr. Robert Kegan (social and moral development)

- Dr. James W. Fowler III (religious development)

- Dr. Jane Loevinger (ego development)

- Sri Aurobindo (spiritual development)

- Dr. Abraham Maslow (human development)

- Dale Carnegie (social skills)

- Dave Ramsey (financial freedom)

- Chris Thomas (decluttering your spaces)

- Margot Anand (tantric sexual practices and theory)

- KRS-One (manifesting, connecting to the Silent Observer, creating your reality)

- Spencer Johnson (facing reality and optimizing it)

- Yogani (meditation techniques, developing practice routines and the nature of dichotomy in the universe)

- Ray Dalio (developing principles)

- Richard Carlson, Ph.D. (eliminating worry)

- Don Miguel Ruiz (principles - the four agreements)

- James Altucher and Claudia Azula Altucher (standing up for yourself, protecting your time and priorities, and how to say NO.)

- Henry David Thoreau (minimalism, questioning social and societal rules and perspective on nature)

- Charlie Hoehen (eliminating stress and mild depression or anxiety)

- Ori Brafman and Rom Brafman (making better decisions)

- Elisabeth Kubler-Ross, M.D. and David Kessler (wisdom from the elderly)

- Mark Manson (not taking things so seriously and not caring what people think)

- Greg McKeown (essentialism)

- Patrick Rhone (minimalism and being satisfied with what you have)

- Ralph Potts (travel and releasing yourself from societal rules)

- Steven Pressfield (the process of creativity and defeating the negative voice)

- Jon Kabatt Zinn (mindfulness and meditation)

- Elle Luna (exploring purpose)

- Wim Hof (breathing techniques and controlling immune and emotional response)

- Eckhart Tolle (connecting to the moment)

- Robert Lanza, MD (effect of human consciousness on the universe)

- Steven Weinberg (the science of the first three minutes post Big Bang)

- Tony Robbins (self mastery)

- Gabriel Wyner (language learning and efficient memorization)

- Jordan Harbinger (social interaction and starting over after crisis)

- Robert Greene (the true nature of humanity in all stages)

- His Holiness The Dalai Lama (compassion and oneness)

- Father Thomas Merton (spiritual and religious development)

- Father Thomas Keating (spiritual and religious development)

- Judith Orloff (connecting to intuition and the body)

- Joe Navarro (dangerous personalities found in stages three and five)

- Pamela Miles (Reiki)

- Ryan Holiday (connecting to challenges and overcoming ego)

- Marcus Aurelius (stoicism)

- Seneca The Younger (stoicism)

- Simon Sinek (human nature and motivation)

- Religious Texts (the nature of humanity, life and the universe):

  - The Bible

  - The Torah

  - The Tao Te Ching

  - The Vedas

  - The Qur'an

  - The Bhagavad Gita

  - The Dhammapada

Your Destination Is Unique …

The Road To Get There Is NOT

Reflecting on my own journey, I wondered if what I went through was unique. I found it was not at all unique. I found that many before me had documented stages of human development and suggested a series of stages that we all go through. Keagan documented social stages. Fowler documented religious stages. Loevinger documented ego stages. Then I did my own digging around. Clearly, people like the Dalai Lama. Mother Theresa, Ghandi, Mandela, and other significant figures had gotten much farther. What were their additional stages? In the end, I found that **each of these sets of stages had significant overlap and linked up nicely to form a single coherent cyclical path of development.** Let's look at the pieces.

Each of us here in the human experience develops along the same path from birth.

Although your hopes and dreams and the life you ultimately want to craft for yourself are completely unique to you, what you are experiencing right now in your desire for self-development is not unique. You are in great company. Each of us here in the human experience develops along the same path from birth.

Maslow's Hierarchy Of Needs

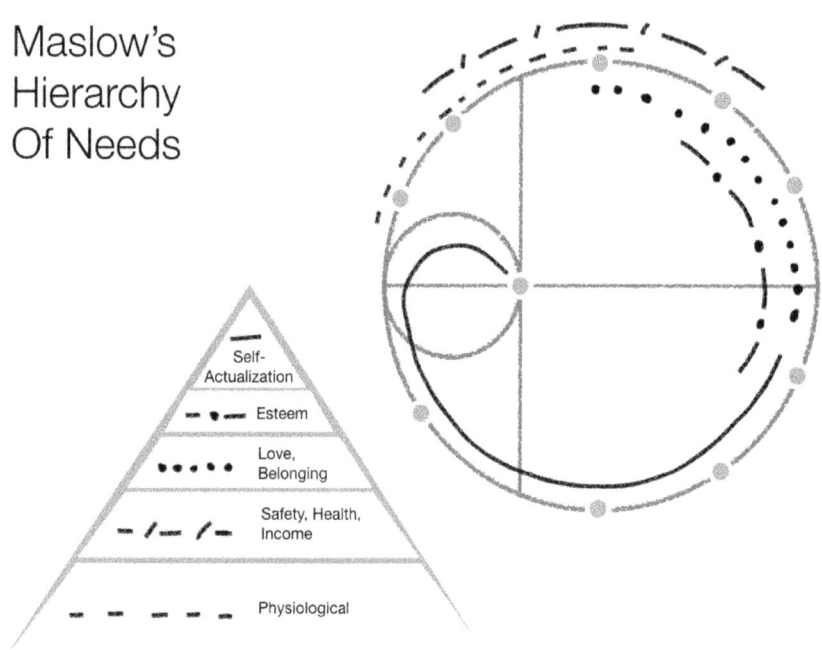

You are probably familiar with Maslow's Hierarchy of Needs. It maps into stages of development as seen here. Maslow's physiological needs correspond to stages two through four, safety, health and income correspond to stages three through five. Love and belonging are found in stages four through six, and so on. They are color coded here.

The Chakra System

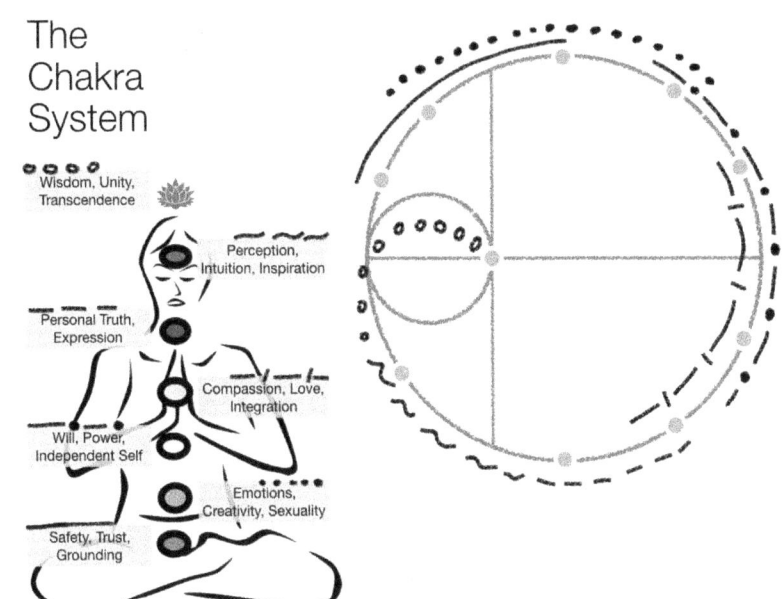

- Wisdom, Unity, Transcendence
- Perception, Intuition, Inspiration
- Personal Truth, Expression
- Compassion, Love, Integration
- Will, Power, Independent Self
- Emotions, Creativity, Sexuality
- Safety, Trust, Grounding

The chakra system is another widely known concept. Chakras are energy centers throughout the body thought to be linked to specific concepts like safety, compassion, expression, etc. The chakras also map to Maslow's hierarchy and to a development process as seen here.

The Shoulders of Giants - Stages Of Human Development

Many other psychologists and thought leaders had similar ideas, each detailing portions of a larger cycle of development. Seen here are just a few of the more prominent names and where their work fits in.

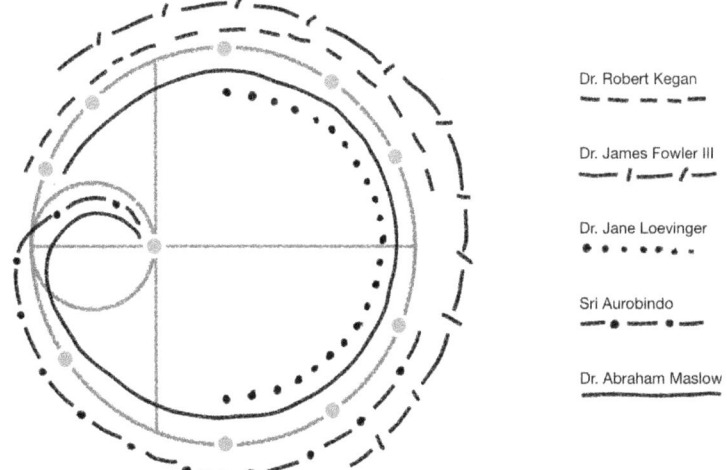

- Dr. Robert Kegan
- Dr. James Fowler III
- Dr. Jane Loevinger
- Sri Aurobindo
- Dr. Abraham Maslow

We see specific themes within their work that suggest four distinct phases of this cycle. We begin by becoming aware of ourselves, then we become aware of others and their ideas and we compare ourselves to them. We then transition to unifying those ideas, and lastly to unifying ourselves.

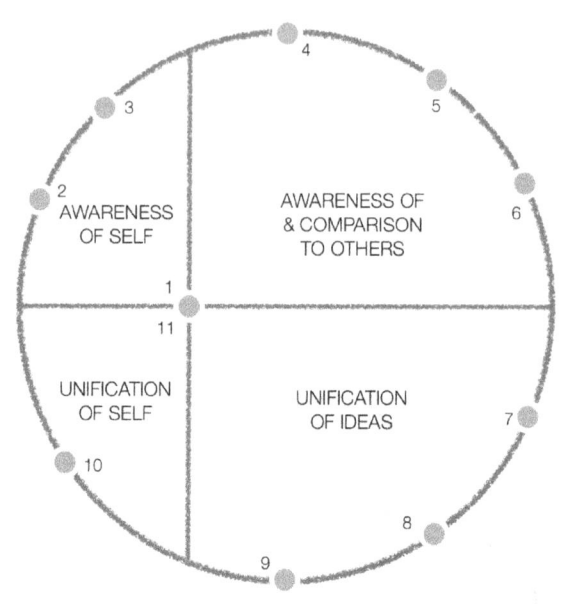

What You Get When You Put It All Together - The Cycle of Human Development

There are eleven stages of development that you CAN experience. (That does not guarantee you will.)

Almost everyone wakes up at some point in their lives (usually between stages five and six). Some call it a midlife crisis, or a quarter-life crisis. Some people wake up much later and some not at all. Some wake up and decide to not take the journey and essentially go back to sleep. Earlier stages are not lesser; in fact, they are essential and must be completed, or you will keep being pulled back into them again and again. The large majority of people in the western world do not make it past stages five or six and spend most of their days there, happily enough.

There are eleven stages of development that you CAN experience; picking up the pieces and complete stages as we revisit them again and again over the course of our lives.

These eleven stages are not a staircase or a straight line of milestones to be achieved. They are not a race for achievement. They are a circle - a cycle of human development that we traverse over and over, trying to pick up the pieces and complete stages as we revisit them again and again over the course of our lives. **Even as you spend more time in later stages, you will periodically be pulled back to earlier stages by major life events** (injury, family issues, elections, etc). You cannot avoid coming around the cycle again and again. But you can spend a lot less time in these earlier stages where life is hard and negative emotions dominate; and you can spend a lot more time in later stages where life is easy, joyous, fulfilling and peaceful.

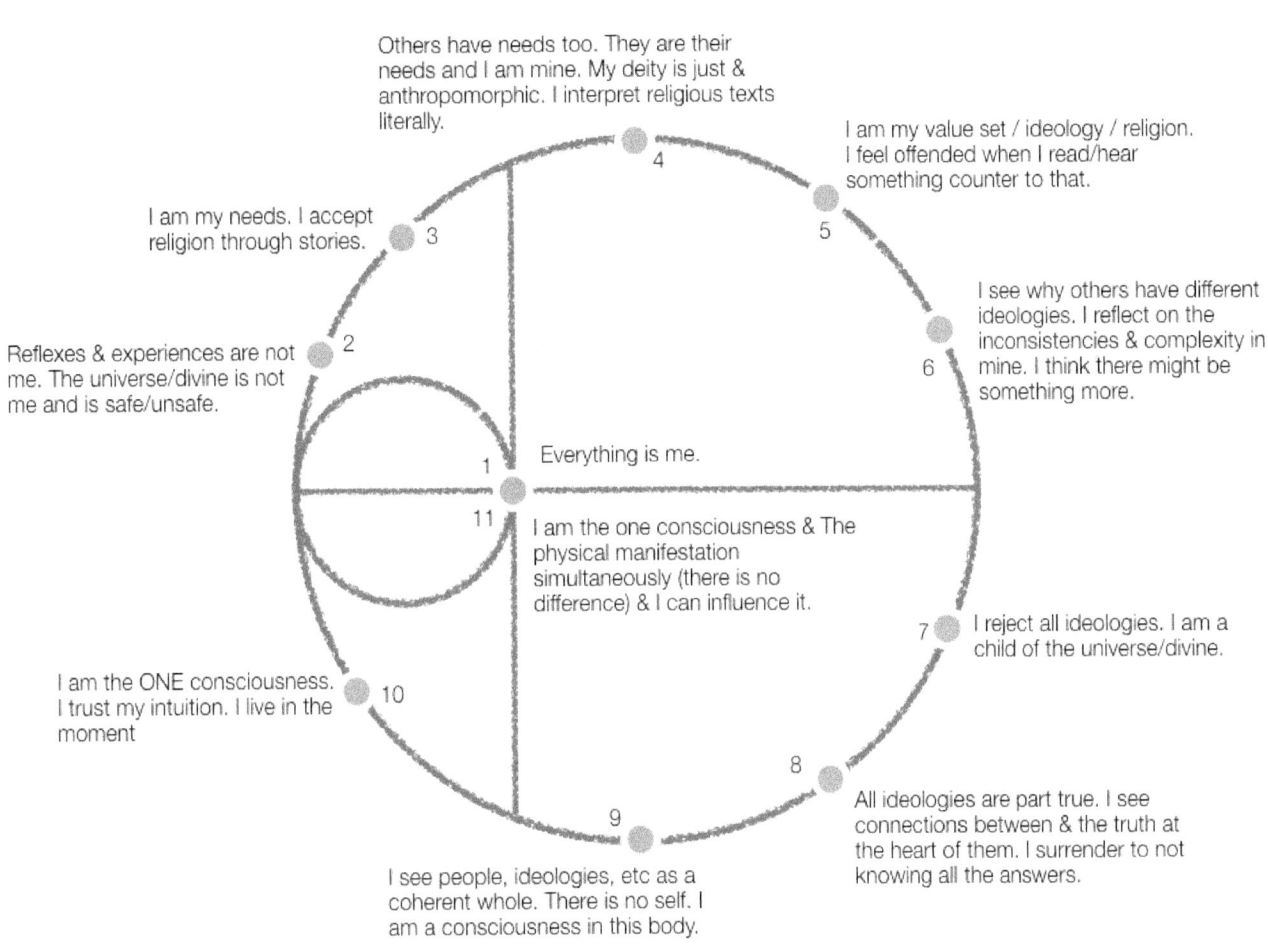

You might ...

(1) work through the tasks, and then

(2) enjoy the recommended reading and podcasts, and then

(3) answer the questions to fuel your thinking.

Stage one and stage eleven are essentially the same (with some added richness). **The irony that we enter this world with the right idea and then must work our way back to it, is rather funny.** The universe has a sense of humor.

Ask yourself: which stage do you find yourself in most of the time? As you go through your day, try to step back from yourself and see where you are on this cycle. Some days, you might traverse the entire cycle in one day. Other days might find you specifically in one stage or another.

Based on the stage where you tend to spend the most time, you have some work to do. **Each stage has a set of important tasks** that must be addressed and questions that you can use to help complete that stage and move yourself to the next. If you leave something undone in one stage, you can be guaranteed that life will bring you back there again soon to keep working. So be proactive yet patient about it and try to complete each stage's tasks as you go.

It is most efficient to start from the beginning and pick up any pieces you have left undone in earlier stages. Most adults wake up between stages five and six, but have significant tasks still to do from stages one through four. Leaving these tasks undone means you will be pulled back to these stages instead of moving forward. It will delay your development. So start at Stage One.

What follows is a roadmap for each stage's characteristics, tasks, recommended reading and some helpful questions. **It helps to keep a journal (on paper or otherwise) to track your thinking and progress**. There are nuances to these tasks so it is worth reading as much material from as many authors as you can to help you in each stage. To that end, There are recommended books in each stage that I have personally found helpful. You should also seek out other books, blogs, and podcasts to give you as much perspective as possible. The key is to read the right books and do the right exercises, asking the right questions, at the right point in the cycle. But if you find that a different order to things works better for you, do not hesitate to make your own best method.

The Key To Your Journey - CONNECTION

Now that we have the cycle and we understand a bit about the stages, the big question is HOW do we move from one stage to another? HOW do we efficiently, effectively and permanently shift perspectives? What is the catalyst that makes someone go from one stage to the next?

The answer to all of those questions is: CONNECTION. Connection means many things. It means being present with, acknowledging, taking ownership of, responsibility for, and forming a deep relationship with the thing in question.

Progressing from one stage to another, or remaining in later stages is a matter of connecting to some aspect of yourself, others, your life, your money, your purpose, your body, your thoughts, ... IN THE RIGHT ORDER. In the roadmap that follows, specific tasks and exercises will guide you through exactly how to do that.

If you focus on forming and maintaining connection, your evolution through the stages will happen on its own. Just focus on connection.

Connection means being present with, acknowledging, taking ownership of, responsibility for, and forming a deep relationship with the thing in question.

The Symbol - Something To Help You Focus On Connection

The symbol developed for this process is based on the four quarters mentioned above, on the eleven stages, the uniqueness of stages one and eleven, and on the many beautiful religious symbols in the world today. You can easily find your favorite symbol inside this one, from the Christian cross to the Muslim moon. You can draw the Star of David between the points or just as easily connect the dots to make the Buddhist symbol for Om. It provides a simple, beautiful, unified symbol that helps you chart your path, remember important lessons, and stay on track. Connect your religion to this symbol to increase your commitment, or meditate on the symbol to set your intentions with or without religion. It has so many uses, you are sure to find a way to use it that suits your journey specifically and accelerates your efforts. It comes in many variations and you can even make your own version. Seen here are just a few variations that have been useful reminders for myself and my students. Simply seeing the symbol can remind you to spend this day in a beautiful state, connect more deeply with others or just honor your commitment to yourself to go to the gym. Use it in any way it may serve you.

 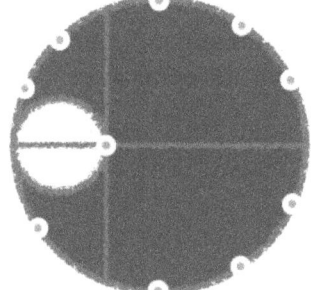 

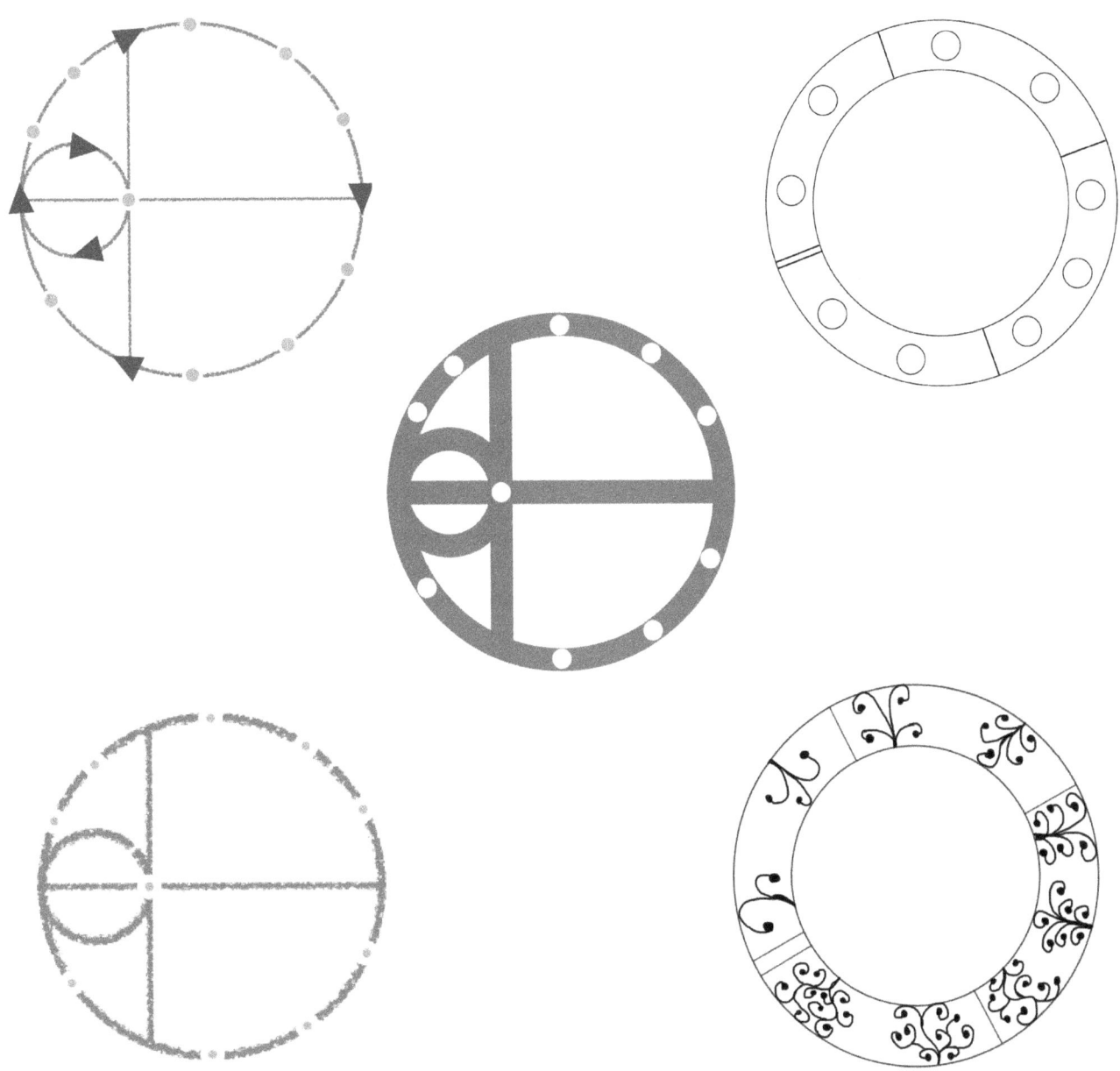

A Private Journey

Your personal journey of self discovery is a critical life long pursuit. It is one of the most profound efforts you will ever undertake. Periodically, it will occupy your whole being. Ironically, or perhaps in perfect balance... nobody cares. The reality is that nobody cares about your journey as they are much too wrapped up in their own equally profound self discovery and rediscovery.

That is great news because it means there is nothing you can really "discover" about your temporary little self that will be all that big of a deal to anyone. For those that know you, they probably already saw in you what you just figured out. And for those who don't know you, they just do not care. So be who you like, do what you want, be who you want - it doesn't matter! That's freedom!

But it gets better... **The journey of self discovery is so critical because it is critical to reach the ultimate and most important conclusion about yourself - that THERE IS NO SELF.**

We spend decades labeling our selves, crafting our selves, honing self images and self presentations. While certainly a fun amusement, these crafted selves serve as little more than adaptations, They help us navigate our present situation socially, politically and financially and understand our current place in the world.

We peel the onion of our "true selves"; celebrating each layer we find and declaring anew that this layer is our true self... no, THIS LAYER is my true self. No, wait. THIS ONE! Until one day when we reach the vacant center and realize that our true self is no-self. Or more precisely, our true self is THE ONENESS - that oneness that is in all of us; not a separate self.

In that moment it strikes us that the "self" as we have been trying to define it for so very long is just a series of temporary manifestations; fleeting costumes tried on and evolved.

If we look around us we will see that everyone else that we have been trying to label and judge and identify is just exactly like us: wholly occupied by peeling away each temporary layer of self to vehemently defend the layer below.

If we look around us we will see that everyone else that we have been trying to label and judge and identify is just exactly like us: wholly occupied by peeling away each temporary layer of self to vehemently defend the layer below. Each of us, however, eventually arrives at the reality in our own time; some not until their last day on this Earth, and some much younger.

We wake up to a world where we are no longer trapped in the need to define a temporary self for ourselves or anyone else. We are at last free to really look around us, no longer occupied by the futile pursuit of what does not even exist - your self. We wake up to the freedom to pursue making a difference, or making something beautiful, or making someone happy... or any number of things that bring joy to the oneness inside us and others.

But this is a private journey; each of us to ourselves. Please do not be disappointed if others are not mesmerized by your journey. They are too busy with their own. However, If you can find others actively working this roadmap, they may be a community of support and resources for you.

Before You Begin - Physical, Mental and Financial Safety

Establish your own safety. **If you are not in a safe environment physically, mentally or financially, you need to change that immediately.**

If you are being abused physically or mentally, be it verbal or emotional or psychological, LEAVE NOW. Do a bit of planning to take your children and yourself to a safe environment. Take all the money and other necessities you can manage and GO. You may think at this moment that you are not strong enough, but you are. We all are. You have no idea how beautiful life can be on the other side of your fear. Please contact family, friends, the police as needed, local organizations or even your doctor (any doctor for that matter). All of these people can help you get out and establish a safe environment where you can craft a beautiful life without fear.

If your finances are a mess, gather a small emergency fund as fast as possible; just enough to handle a major car repair. Sell everything, get a second job (or a third) but make this happen FAST before you begin this process. Why? Because self development is next to impossible when you live in fear of the next car repair or other financial issue. This is Dave Ramsey's "baby step #1." It puts you more at ease while you get the rest of your life together (finance and all).

You have no idea how beautiful life can be on the other side of your fear.

LET'S GO!

Once you have established physical, mental and financial basic safety, you are ready to get started. **Start from Stage One and work through any tasks and questions that you have not already done, any that you have not done in a long time, and any that you think you could do better.** Take your time. Contemplate these questions and concepts. Give them time to evolve you. If you do the tasks, and really think about the results, you will see immediate progress. Track it in your journal.

Stage One: Everything Is Me

Confounded
We are found
Educated in emergence
One with the separateness
Reveling in existence
Drenched
In our connectedness
To love purely
Convinced
In our openness
That we do not know

Characteristics

- A newborn infant, or like a newborn infant.
- Other people are not separate from you.
- Your experiences define you.

Challenges

When you are in this stage, you can tend to obsess over the stories of your past and present; times when you were wronged. You can tend to focus on describing your current situation (for the story you will tell about it later), rather than making conscious choices about what you want your situation to be and taking action to change it. You can also feel overwhelmed at the journey ahead of you.

Tasks

Grounding Yourself...

☐ Declutter your schedule, your attention and your spaces to focus on this process.

☐ Choose a form of meditation or prayer. Set aside some time each day and hold it sacred.

Learning To Trust...

☐ Understand the emotional roots of your choices.

☐ Learn to trust yourself.

☐ Learn to trust the Universe/River/Divine.

RESOURCES

- *Radical Acceptance* by Tara Brach
- *Deep Meditation* by Yogani
- *You Have Too Much Shit* by Chris Thomas
- *The Power of No* by James Altucher and Claudia Azula Altucher
- *Essentialism* by Greg McKeown
- *Enough* by Patrick Rhone

QUESTIONS TO FUEL YOUR THINKING

- What experiences have shaped you? In what ways?

- What did you learn from these experiences? About yourself, about others, about the world, about life? Do you think these lessons are true?

- Was there a time when you acted out of reflex? Are you the human animal that acted? Or the witness inside?

- Within each of these experiences, consider each person involved - can you see their humanity? (if not, it's OK...).

- Within each of your experiences, can you see YOUR humanity? What were the emotional roots of your choices and actions? Be honest. How did it turn out?

- Can you see that you are not your experiences?

Grounding Yourself - Connecting To Your Time, Attention And Spaces

Feeling grounded means feeling like you have a stable place to operate from. This stable place might be a particular physical space like a room or home. It is even more important, however, that you have a sense of being grounded in your time, your attention and in an internal space. **Being internally grounded is a feeling of self-reliance, or of being complete unto yourself.** It is not dependent on anyone else's presence or affirmation. It is not dependent on your job, where you live, or what relationship (if any) you are currently in. Being grounded in yourself is a stable foundation even when life, relationships, home, work or other areas seem unstable. The three most important aspects to start with are: time, attention and spaces (both internal and external).

We are lucky to have a lot of resources in this life: food, clothing, shelter, friends, family, money, etc. You can find more food. You can get more clothes. If you have to, you can find new friends. You can even make more money. But **you cannot get more time and you cannot expand your attention.**

Your time on this earth is finite. You cannot know how many days you have left, but you do know that it is limited. Within each of those days, your capacity to hold things in your attention is also limited. As such, your time and attention are the only fixed, non-renewable resources that you have. You have a certain amount and you cannot get more. Therefore you are wise to guard your time and attention more closely than you guard your possessions and your money. Think about how vehemently we guard our possessions and our money. Entire industries exist around guarding your stuff and your finances. But we will let anyone and anything take our time and attention.

You cannot be everything to everyone but everyone will be happy to make sure you are nothing to anyone.

We all know that time is a limited resource. But we seldom act like it. It often takes a major crisis in our lives to truly internalize the fact that our time on this earth is limited and we do not know when it will end. Maybe tomorrow. Maybe decades from now. We find ourselves so willing to let anyone and anything take our time to the point that we do not spend any time on what we ourselves want to be doing. If this sounds familiar, you already know that you need to make time for your own health, pursuits, joys, hobbies, purpose, and self-evolution. If you are not doing that yet, then step one is to clear your schedule. You cannot be everything to everyone but everyone will be happy to make sure you are nothing to anyone.

Think of your time like currency. What do you spend it on? What does that get you? Actively examine each hour of your day and demand return on that investment. It cannot return more time so it will have to return something else - joy, connection, inspiration, creativity, money, opportunities, growth, etc. Some hours are best spent on earning money. Some are best spent on sleep, mediation or prayer, exercise, or other self care. Some hours are best spent forwarding your personal goals, learning new skills, experiencing life, and filling your soul. Demand that things compete for your time.

If you are not yet independently wealthy (don't laugh, you can get there), and you still need to work to put food on the table and pay the rent, then it goes without saying that you will need to make time to work; perhaps a lot of time to work. Working long hours, however, does not stop you from making some time each day for the reading, thinking, writing, exercising, meditating, praying, creating, taking classes or other activities that will accelerate your development and your connection to every aspect of your life. At least one hour per day is recommended and more is always better.

Step One - find one hour each day to work on you.

Recognizing that you need to work, eat, shower, take care of children, and so forth, there are still likely a lot of ways you might be spending your limited time in ways that do not do anything for you. Does watching videos do anything for you? Maybe; if they are the right kind of videos. Other time wasters include reading headlines, watching TV, playing the wrong games, reading the wrong things and so on. That is not to say that down time spent on meaningless activity is all bad. But if you need an hour to work on you, you can find it here among your daily time wasters.

Your attention is even more limited. Within each day we have, according to studies by Nelson Cowan, Jeff Rouder and Richard Morey, a maximum of seven things that we can carry in our conscious attention. But it is really, they report, more like four. There are some things that our brains are always tracking such as physical safety, bodily functions and our immediate environment. Then we laden our conscious and subconscious attention with so much more: work, kids, spouses, home repairs, the dog needs to be walked, don't forget to do the laundry, worries about politics, social issues, and people we don't even know but we heard about.

Everything we own, everything we spend our time on, all the expectations that we put on ourselves and others, the roles we play, ... They all take up residence in our attention. Every pair of pants in your closet owns a tiny bit of real estate in your attention. Every vehicle you own, every square foot of house that you live in, and every little tweet, post, article, and headline that you consume. **Anything and everything in your reality is taking up bits of your attention.**

The thing is... It's a conscious choice. That's YOUR attention and YOU decide what lives there. It's time you took it back.

For most people, the problem is having too many things to do in a day and too many people, places and things clambering for your attention. You might like to make space for self-development, life-optimization, finding peace, finding your purpose and carrying out that purpose, etc.

Freedom of attention creates freedom of intention, and freedom of time lets you make that intention real. In other words, **your attention is open to inspiration and your time is open to make it happen.**

So how can you declutter your time and attention? First, think of it as a competition. That is, activities must compete for your time, and people, places and things must compete for your attention. "But they already do," you shout!! Yes, they do. And you need to set the bar a LOT higher. **If you currently feel overwhelmed, it is because your time and attention are like a public bathroom - anyone can show up and use them how they please.** As a result, it is a real mess, largely created by others but you get to clean it up. You need to elevate your standards of admission, get a velvet rope and a bouncer, and turn your time and attention into the most exclusive, peaceful resort imaginable. Very few people, places, things and activities are allowed in and they must have a really good reason to be there.

Let the competition begin. Start with an 80/20 analysis. Get some paper and write down the 20% of your daily activities that bring you 80% of the joy, or the growth, or the progress towards your goals, etc. Who are the 20% of the people in your life that bring you 80% of the annoyance and grief? Read up on Pareto's Law in Tim Ferriss's blog and other places and try applying it to everything. What is the 20% of your stuff that brings you 80% of the use, joy, etc? You get the idea.

Start with an 80/20 analysis.

Next, say NO.

Then act on it. Remove the people, places, things, and activities that cause you grief, sadness, more work, annoyance, or just do not contribute. I know, that will include your kids and you can't get rid of your kids, BUT you CAN reduce how much attention they require once they are of a certain more independent age (old enough to do their own laundry, help with the cooking, and eventually drive themselves to all those events). **When removing people from your world, it is often better to avoid drama and just slowly, quietly fade away.** Use your best judgement.

Next, say NO. Say no (kindly) to your boss, to your spouse, to your kids (especially your kids), to your neighbor, and to the local organizations that want your time and attention. Stop saying no to yourself. That is, start saying yes to yourself first, and then to others. Martyrdom does not make you important, respected, or at peace. Your suffering does not prevent the suffering of others, it multiplies it. You need to get your own self in order before you can help anyone else. **The world does not need your burned out, half-hearted "help".** Fill your soul so that you have something to give. You will be pleasantly shocked and amazed at how little anyone cares that you said no. You will be equally amazed at how much the average person understands, and how people at work, at home and around town will start to respect you, and value your time and attention because you do. See James Altucher's book, *The Power of NO* for how to do this kindly and effectively.

Once you stop letting other people control your time and attention, you will have the challenge of your own efforts and desires competing for it. There are so many fascinating things in this world that you could pursue: travel, work or business, language, learning, reading, volunteering, playing with your kids and grandkids, finding and chasing your purpose... It will come down to prioritizing the things that YOU want to use your time and attention for.

The connection priority:
- body
- self
- others
- world;
in that order.

Start with anything that maintains your connection to your body - sleep, food, movement, sunlight, self care, etc. These needs are paramount and the foundation of your ability to focus on anything at all. **Next, maintain your connection to yourself** through experiences, self-development, etc. Third, add in things that connect you to **your world and others**. That makes the priority: body, self, others, world; in that order.

As a simple rule, if someone else can do it better, faster or cheaper, maybe they should, and you should not. If someone else would take more joy in it, let them. If it would be a point of growth for someone else, give it to them.

As you progress, don't forget to defend your time and attention. This requires ongoing maintenance. People in stage three will always try to make you think it is your responsibility to give them what they want, help them, solve their problems, or take their work load. People in other stages are sometimes just lazy. It's not that helping people is off the menu, it's that **helping others should be from the perspective of your purpose or passion** (because that is where you are most effective), and only after you maintain yourself.

As a simple rule, if someone else can do it better, faster or cheaper, maybe they should, and you should not. If someone else would take more joy in it, let them. If it would be a point of growth for someone else, give it to them.

How will you clear out your time and attention? What tasks can you take off your plate?

Next, consider a major clean-out of everything you own. If you have things you don't use or don't want, give them away or sell them to someone who could use them. Good books along these lines include: The *Life Changing Magic Of Tidying Up*, *Essentialism*, and *You Have Too Much Shit*. Get inspired and get going. For your work spaces, where you have less influence, you can remove distracting elements and bring in items that give you a sense of peace, joy, focus, or any other feeling you would like to have at work. If you work in a factory, restaurant or other setting where changing things is not an option, focus on your inner space and carry it with you.

Lastly, let's talk about that internal space. This is where you want to anchor yourself. Creating a place of peace inside you means you always have somewhere to go regardless of how chaotic the outside world becomes or where you find yourself. **You can be your own place of certainty and peace.**

Take a few minutes to try this: close your eyes, breathe deeply and let it out slowly. Consider what your body feels like. How does your head feel? What can you hear? Can you feel your heart beating? Can you feel your lungs breathing? Feel gratitude for that. What does it feel like in your belly? Take some time to mentally explore every space inside yourself as you ask yourself what it feels like. Somewhere in there is your place of peace. It might be your heart, or a particular spot in your belly, or your lungs. Somewhere in there feels like peace; like a secret place you can retreat to anytime you like. For most people it is deep in the belly in a place called the lower dantian, but it could be any space that feels like home for you. To carry a place of certainty within yourself is the ultimate defense against a chaotic world. Find your internal space and return there daily, or whenever you need it.

Take some time to mentally explore every space inside yourself as you ask yourself what it feels like. Somewhere in there is your place of peace.

Forms Of Mediation And Prayer

Prayer is often thought of as a form of ingratiating the divine or asking the divine for what you want and perhaps for guidance. Meditation can include that, and also includes a very important extra ingredient - listening for the answer. There are many forms of mediation and prayer to try. You may have grown up reciting particular prayers. There is no need to abandon that. Consider, instead, adding some new forms in just to try them. Be experimental and see what works for you. The following list is just a start. Add your own variations as you find them.

Forms of Prayer...

- **Specific Prayers For Specific Occasions** - these are recited the same way every time such as blessing a meal. Use the ones you know or make your own, specific to your situation.

- **Sending Gratitude** - connect with the divine and give thanks for everything wonderful in your life. You might speak it out loud or just in your mind. Feel the gratitude in your heart and send it to the divine.

- **Asking** - connect with the divine to make a request. Ask for what you want and then give over your desire for it to the divine, trusting that the divine will deliver it, if it is in your best interests.

- **Contemplation** - quietly contemplate a thought, question or quote from your favorite religious or other text as if you are contemplating it together with the divine. Insight and guidance often comes during this type of prayer.

Connect to the divine, ask for the help you need and don't forget to be quiet long enough to hear the answer.

Forms of Meditation...

There are so many forms of mediation that are worth exploring. Search on types of mediation, research each for more detail, and make your own based on these categories or others. Feel free to combine methods into each session. For example, you might begin by focusing on the breath, then focus on the silence and ask for guidance, and then end with manifestation. Use whatever combination works for you.

- Clearing The Mind By **Focusing On Something Else**...

  - Focus on a **word or sound**.

  - Focus on your **breathing**.

- Focus on specific places within the **body** and how they feel.

- Focus on what is happening in and around you in **this moment**.

- Focus on the **silence** - this is the ultimate goal of most forms of mediation. It can be challenging to achieve so it helps to warm up by focusing on something else first such as the breath, and then, when the mind is more calm, rest in the silence. This is usually when answers and guidance come. Feel free to ask the universe / divine what you want to know such as how to solve a challenge or the answer to a particular question.

- **Manifesting** (Asking For What You Want)

  - **Samyama** - Think of what you want, then take your desire for it and drop it into the infinite silence inside you, knowing that if it forwards your purpose, it will of course be granted.

  - **Feeling-Based Manifestation** - Imagine how it feels to already have what you want. Visualize it lightly in the back of your mind.

- **Loving Kindness** - send love to yourself, those your care about, friends, neighbors, ... work your way outward to sending love and good wishes to people you do not like, those who have wronged you, and even further out to the world and the universe.

- **Guided Meditation** - there are many wonderful mediations led by trained teachers who guide you through what to do. If you are not yet ready to mediate on your own, try seeking a guided mediation on a mediation app, on your favorite streaming service or on various podcasts.

Making It Your Own...

If you are religious, you can combine prayer and meditation techniques to feel more connected to the divine and to nurture that relationship. If you are spiritual, but not religious, you can combine these techniques for that same connection outside of institutionalized religion. And if you are neither spiritual nor religious, you can still learn to quiet the mind and connect to the universe and all the answers it has to offer.

Play with techniques, combine techniques, and experiment to find the right combination of prayer and/or mediation for you.

You can read about many interesting mediation techniques (and I recommend it), but do not think that you must follow each to infinite detail. That is why I have presented them in such generality here. Play with techniques, combine techniques, and experiment to find the right combination of prayer and/or mediation for you. They key in all of these is to quiet the mind. That is, to simply sit down, shut up and listen. How you get to that state of a quiet, listening mind is not important. The practice of getting there is what matters and is what will bring you the most benefit. This is liberating. Developing your own ceremony, ritual or routine that is optimized for your own benefit will play a major role in accelerating your evolution through the stages towards complete connection with every aspect of your life.

Connecting to yourself is a great place to start. Here you are. Inhabiting this body on this planet, in this amazing life. But your SELF is something else. Your SELF is something deeper inside. Connecting to yourself will include connecting to many facets. Take them one at a time and find joy in the exploration and connection as you get to know the real you.

Connecting To The Emotional Roots Of Your Choices

Major decisions in your life come in many forms... marriage, starting a business, ending a business, changing jobs, changing careers, going back to school, etc. Often we can get our decision down to two options and then we struggle. Not wanting to make a mistake, we are paralyzed in the last step of deciding. What follows is a method for making these decisions that is so revealing that the decision makes itself.

First, list each option across the top of a page so it will have a dedicated column and you can compare them when you are done. Your options might be as simple as yes and no, or something more complicated.

For each option, ask yourself WHY you should pick that option. List your reasons out, as many as come to you. Try to be really honest with yourself here about why you are drawn to that option. Make your best possible argument for each option. Really sell it to yourself.

Then, for each reason why, boil it down to the one word emotional trigger that is at the root of that reason: greed, fear, ego, purpose, service, joy, love, hate, etc. Be brutally honest.

When you get down to two options and just cannot decide, it is because **your human mind (greed, ego, fear, hate, etc) is arguing with your soul (purpose, service, joy, love)** and the answer will be shockingly clear. If you choose the option based on negative emotions, you will have a negative outcome. If you choose the option based on positive emotions, you will have a positive outcome. Why? Because your actions will ultimately multiply the emotion that drives them.

Think back on big decisions you have made in your life. What were the true emotional triggers for those decisions? How did it turn out for you? When did it go well? When did it go poorly? Are there patterns you can see?

List your choices.

List your reasons.

What is the emotional root of each reason?

The right choice is based on positive emotions.

It is really that simple. What big decision have your been trying to make? What are the emotional roots of each side? Which side should you choose?

Trusting Yourself

Trusting yourself is a phrase that is thrown around often. Here, we mean trusting the silent observer inside, your intuition, and your ability to understand yourself at a level that lets your truth come out. This is a self you can trust and rely on. Understanding the emotional roots of your choices was step one. Now that you can analyze your thoughts and emotions, it is time to trust yourself in terms of trusting that the questions you have, have answers, even if you cannot know them right now. Trust in your need to explore these questions and others as they arise. Trust in what draws you to want to know more. And trust that your journey will take you to a beautiful place. Trust that your destination is unique but your journey is ancient and well tested. Trust in you inner guide to get you there.

To learn to trust yourself in this way, **start by recalling times when your intuition was right.** Maybe you ignored it, or maybe you followed it, but it was right. Recall times when you were drawn by something deep inside you to take a certain action, and it was right. Can you recognize the difference between being compelled from a deep place of intuition versus impulse from the animal brain? The animal brain can often steer you wrong but your intuition never will. Practice recognizing the difference by thinking back on your past choices. Take your time and find as many examples from your past as you can. Write them down and categorize them as intuition versus animal brain, or true self versus monkey mind. Analyze as many examples as you can find and then look at your list. How often was your true self wrong? Not often, I bet. See the proof that you can trust your true self. Now that you can discern between compelling from the true self and impulse from the monkey mind, you can trust your human mind to see the difference and follow the path of the true self. **This is not a blind trust, but a trust built on a track record of leading you on the right path.**

From now on, when you feel drawn to do something, take a moment to note how it feels. Does this feel like a compelling from your soul? Or does this feel like impulse from the monkey mind? What is the emotional root of this? Take your time and train yourself further. As time goes on, your ability to discern between impulse and compelling will grow stronger and only increase the trust that you have in your true inner self.

The animal brain can often steer you wrong but your intuition never will. Practice recognizing the difference by thinking back on your past choices.

Trusting Your River / Universe / The Divine

The river of your life is a metaphor for how we seem to have a combination of fate and free will guiding our lives. Have you noticed that sometimes life seems like a struggle? And sometimes things just seem to work out easily? Your river wants to take you towards your purpose (whatever that may be, and however that may change over time). When you are on track towards your purpose, you will find that life flows easily. But if you struggle against your river, that is, away from your purpose, life seems hard.

Learning to trust your river is not easy. We cannot see around the next corner and the journey towards our purpose usually includes several leaps of faith. It can be so very hard to just close your eyes and go with it. Once you recognize the nature of your river, however, it becomes not just easy, but a relief to let your river take you where you need to be.

Consider the experiences, good and bad, that have influenced you, shaped you or been significant in your life in some way. You know what they are. Write them down. Consider how they influenced you. What did they teach you? What gifts did they have for you? (skills, perspective, joy, love, fear, …). Appreciate all of these experiences for what they taught you (especially the hard lessons), and for any joy or love that they brought you. Appreciate them for the gifts they gave you.

Now let them go. They are in the past. **You HAVE experiences and you LEARN from experiences but you are NOT your experiences.** You might keep your list that you wrote out above or you might ceremonially burn it, tear it up, throw it out or delete it. Ceremonies and rituals are powerful psychological devices. So if you are having trouble letting go of any particular experience, write it on a piece of paper, thank it for teaching you and giving you skills you can use later, then burn it (safely!) in a bowl or fireplace. Thank your river for that experience and for experiences to come. Reaffirm that you are not this experience or any other. Feel the distance between you and that experience.

New experiences will come along and continue to shape you. Thank them for what they teach you, and let them go, too.

When you can detach from your experiences, and view them as an outside observer, recognizing that they are not you, but they shape you and that is a good thing, then you will find more trust in your river/universe/divine.

> *When you are on track towards your purpose, you will find that life flows easily. But if you struggle against your river, that is, away from your purpose, life seems hard.*

Can you see the river of your life shaping you? Can you see how it guides your choices and teaches you lessons and skills and gives you the gifts of joy, love and occasionally fear, perspective or compassion. Can you see how it is leading you to something? Can you let go and trust in this river/universe/divine?

Trusting your river can be hard because we know from past experience that it may bring you to a place of sadness, loss or fear. But trusting your river has an interesting effect. The more you trust your river, the easier life becomes because you stop struggling. When you flow with your river, it takes you more directly where you need to be. There are fewer places of sadness and fear and when those times come, you have the perspective that this too is being human. Such compassion for yourself and your shared humanity is the key to making sadness and fear dissipate. So by trusting your river, you ultimately minimize the time you spend with these emotions.

When you trust your river, you tend to not act out of fear, jealously, sadness or other negative emotions. **When you trust your river, you act out of love, purpose, joy and other positive emotions.** The result will multiply those positive emotions. So the irony is: to have fewer bad times in your life, you have to stop fearing having bad times in your life. This is an important glimpse into the true nature of life. You get what you think about and feel. If you think about bad situations and you feel those negative emotions, you will get more of them. If you think about good situations and feel those positive emotions, you will get more of those instead.

Trust your river/universe/divine. Trust that your river is taking your where you need to be and that your river has a system to ensure that you can have any life that you want. If you want beautiful and amazing, your river is ready to take you there.

So the irony is: to have fewer bad times in your life, you have to stop fearing having bad times in your life. This is an important glimpse into the true nature of life.

Stage Two: I Am Everything Except Experiences And Reflexes

Body etched
Mind shaped
We are bent
To the reality
Of separate existence
To survive
Long enough
To become
The divine
Oneness
We once were

CHARACTERISTICS

- A young infant or child
- Impulsive
- A sense of the universe or divine as generally safe or unsafe

CHALLENGES

In this stage, you can tend to neglect your needs by simply not knowing what they are. Traumatic events and major life experiences can pull you back to this stage as you try to process what has occurred and detach from it. That takes real effort and your needs can sometimes be neglected because they may have changed.

Tasks

Connect to experiences...

☐ Manifest the experiences you want, understanding that they teach you but are not you.

☐ Don't waste time on the past, except to see how far you have come and to be thankful for that.

Connect to your needs...

☐ Evolve your list of needs as you learn about yourself and grow. Keep this list of needs somewhere close so you can refer to it.

Connect to your body...

☐ Ensure that you are getting enough sleep.

☐ Make time for regenerative activities such as hot baths, time alone, massage, exercise, meditation or prayer, etc.

☐ Start moving. Choose a form of movement and engage with it most days.

Resources

- *Boundaries* by Dr. Henry Cloud and Dr. John Townsend

Questions To Fuel Your Thinking

- What kind of experiences do you want in the future?

- Do you see the universe / your deity as safe or unsafe? Why?

- What are your needs? List them out: physical, nutritional, mental, emotional, intellectual, spiritual, financial, etc.

- Do you really need that? Or are you afraid of something? Why do you need that? Dig deep.

Connecting To Experiences

Experiences are one of the first things we learn to separate from ourselves. We inherently know that we should not identify with the bad (or good) things that happen to us. But that is really hard to put into practice. Suppose, for example, that you had been robbed while walking down the street. You may take on a sense of fear that stays with you for your whole life. If you have experienced an assault, you might hold on to a sense of unworthiness or sense that you are a victim.

These bits of identity weigh us down and stop us from moving forward. Good experiences can be equally stifling if you keep revisiting them over and over. Suppose that in High School you were a great athlete. You might hold on to a notion of high school star that can prevent you from ever doing anything great in your adult life.

Are you holding on to a bit of the past? **Ironically, to let go of an experience, you must connect with it deeply.**

For each major experience in your life, write down what it taught you. What beliefs did it give you about yourself, humanity, or the world? Do you still think those beliefs are correct? What should you carry forward from those experiences?

Those experiences, good and bad, teach you something about yourself, humanity or the world. It is worth examining them for what they have taught you, affirming that they are not you, and then moving on. If you find that you are revisiting the same event over and over, consider getting some help to let it go. Therapy, Reiki, massage, journaling, prayer with a trusted spiritual advisor and other techniques may help you bring it to the surface and let it go. You can also create your own ceremony to let it go. Meanwhile, pack your life with new and exciting events so that you have something else to fill your thoughts.

Don't waste time on the past, except to see how far you have come, what you have learned and to be thankful for that. As new experiences enter your life, thank them for what they have taught you, enjoy recalling them from time to time but let them go too. Focus on the now and plan for your future.

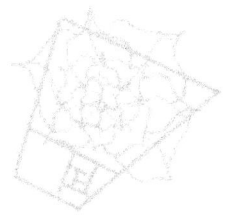
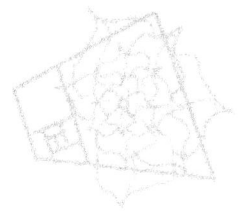
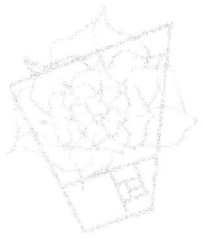
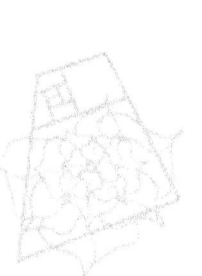

For each major experience in your life, write down...

What it taught you.

What beliefs it gave you.

If you think those beliefs are correct.

And what you will take from it.

Then let it go.

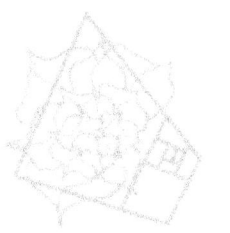

Connecting To Your Needs

Physical

Mental

Spiritual

Medical

Professional

Other

We all have needs. The problem comes when we tend to ignore our needs, or worse, not even know what they are. When moving between phases of your life, your needs will evolve. It is useful to take some time to consider what they are and list them out. Consider each of the following categories and make some more of your own….

Physical Needs - How much sleep do you need? How much down time just relaxing? What kind of exercise do you need? What are your sexual needs? (we will get to that more later as well). What kind of nutrition do you need? What kind of self-care routine is optimal?

Mental/Emotional Needs - Do you need to feed your mind? What kind of intellectual activities do you need? Do you need close relationships? What kind and how much contact? Do you need time alone? How much?

Spiritual Needs - Do you need time to attend to your faith? Time to attend a service of some kind? Or just time to study your favorite text? Are there pilgrimages or retreats that you feel called to take?

Medical Needs - What issues in your body and mind to you need to attend to from a medical perspective? How can you take care of these issues? Can you isolate the root cause or the way out? What time and opportunities do you need to connect with your body and mind to heal?

Professional or Purpose-Driven Needs - What professional training do you need? What time do you need to pursue your purpose? What would you do with that time? What equipment, or skills or knowledge do you need?

What Else? - Your unique life may have other needs. Do you need to feel like a good parent? Do you need to feel validated for something?

The important thing is to be truly honest about what you need. Do not feel ashamed of what you need. If you feel badly about a need or you find that you need something unhealthy, explore that. Why do you feel that way? If you find that you have needs that are unhealthy, ask yourself WHY you need that. What does it do for you? How does it make you feel? You are being rewarded in some way for filling that supposed need. Ask if there are other ways that you can get the same feeling or the same result in a healthier way.

Update your list of needs as you learn about yourself and grow. Make sure you are attending to your needs regularly.

Lastly, remember that needs change. As you evolve and your life evolves, your needs evolve too. Update your list of needs as you learn about yourself and grow. Keep this list near so you can refer to it, and periodically update it. Overall, all of this planing and understanding is meaningless if you do not act. Make sure you are attending to your needs regularly.

Connecting To Your Body - Sleep, Regeneration, And Movement

Connecting to your body ensures that you will make your health and well being a priority, which forms the foundation for connection to yourself, and ultimately everything else.

Sleep. Move. Regenerate. Repeat.

Among your needs that you previously cataloged, will certainly be physical needs like sleep. **Connecting to your body starts with making sure you are getting enough sleep.** How much is enough depends on you. Everyone is different. There is a lot of research out on how much sleep is the optimal amount. You can read about it, or you can just experiment on yourself. Keep a log of how much sleep you get and how you feel the next day. Too little sleep tends to make us feel stressed and impatient. Too much sleep tends to make us feel tired and unmotivated. The right answer is somewhere in the middle.

Beyond sleep, you can connect with your body through **regenerative activities** such as...

- Hot baths (or ice baths)
- Massage
- Exercise or movement (see below)
- Somatic meditation (focused on scanning the body for feelings and sensations)
- Rituals to honor your body (see Margot Anand's writings for ideas)
- Giving yourself a pedicure or other treatment
- Giving yourself Reiki
- Or just being mindful when shaving or brushing your hair or teeth

Regenerative activities should be on your list of needs. If they are not, add some now. Regenerative time, sometimes called self-care is critical to maintaining a connection to your body and therefore to yourself, which is the foundation for everything else. Do not neglect it. Try several different types of regenerative activities and see what gives you the most benefit.

Next, start moving. Your body was not built to stand still or sit down all day. Choose a form of movement and engage with it regularly. Here are some ideas...

Move at the gym...

- Walking
- Running
- Cycling
- Elliptical Training
- Jumping Rope
- Dancing
- Aerobics/Cardio Classes
- Tai Chi
- Martial Arts

Move at home...

- Turn on the radio and dance in your living room.
- Try fitness or dance classes and videos online.
- Do yoga or Tai Chi at home.

Move in the world...

- Walk or run around your neighborhood.
- Hike a nearby trail.
- Kayak a nearby lake or river.

This is just the beginning. Get creative! You do not need to be an athlete, or have impressive photos of your efforts. **Just move.** For five minutes or five hours, it does not matter. The point is to move every day. You may find that some activities are a lot of fun and you may choose to do more of them, or do them with friends. Besides all the documented benefits of movement for your mind, heart and body, movement connects you to your body in a way that lets you appreciate your human form and all it can do.

Connecting to your body through sexuality comes in stage three, so be patient. Get your sleep, regeneration and movement in line first (in that order) so you will be ready.

Manifesting - A Comprehensive And Simple Guide

Step One... What would you like to manifest?
Plan it out in advance. What would enrich your life, your efforts or your wellbeing right now? You can ask for nearly anything. Here are a few categories to get you thinking ...

- People (who are not already in your life)
- Places
- Things
- Lifestyle
- Self-Completeness
- Experiences
- Feelings / Emotional States
- Jobs
- Opportunities
- Health
- Immunity
- Social Interaction
- ... be as creative as you like.

Step Two...Technique: Do it right and you will get what you ask for (see the critical warnings below)

1. **WRITE** it down by hand on paper or in your device.

2. **FEEL** what it's like to have or experience what you want.

3. **LET GO** of your need and desire for it, as if you already have it.

4. **LISTEN** closely for hints and guidance on how to make it happen.

5. **ACT** on that guidance.

6. Keep it up daily - **BE PATIENT** - requests may take days to years.

Critical Warnings:

- The universe/divine attempts to deliver on all requests - so be careful what you wish for.

- Mind your root emotion. Why do you want that? If it is coming from a place of fear, inadequacy, or other negative emotion, you will get it in a way that multiplies that negative emotion. It will make it worse. Likewise, if you are coming from a place of love, compassion, purpose, joy, etc, you will get your answer in a way that multiplies these emotions instead.

- Once a person, place or thing is in your life, you cannot change their qualities. You can only add or remove things from your life, so plan carefully.

- When attracting people, who you get is also looking for you. Be careful to assess WHY they are looking for you.

- Be specific... very specific ... or you may get undesirable variations.

- Once you are experienced, It is possible to manifest things without really meaning to. Be mindful of your thoughts and feelings.

- If what you want is somehow bad for you, the river of your life will try to stop you by making it a struggle to get what you want. Pay attention to that and stop chasing it. Your river is trying to save you from pain and suffering but will ultimately let you have that pain, if you insist.

- Understand that manifesting can feel like you are in control. You do not have control. What you have is influence over that which is not yet in your reality. Do not confuse influence for control.

Most beginners make the mistake of not feeling what it is like to have it. Vision boards are useless if you do not feel it. Feeling is everything. If you feel it, it will come.

Overall, have fun! Manifesting is the mechanism by which you will design your ideal life and make it real. There is no better time to start than now.

Vision boards are useless if you do not feel it. Feeling is everything. If you feel it, it will come.

Manifesting Struggle - Swimming Against Your River

Our thoughts manifest our reality - you can, simply by thinking about what you want and feeling what it would be like to have it, bring people, places, things, jobs, situations, etc, into your life. You can design and create your self and your world. So, why then does it sometimes not work? Why it is sometimes such a struggle?

The universe makes an effort to deliver on what you ask for, BUT sometimes it may try to stop you, for your own good. IF you are asking for something counter to your purpose, you will struggle. And if you ask for something that is massively counter to your purpose, the universe may block it all together.

They key is to recognize this struggle.

Trust that the universe will try to block you from anything that would destroy your purpose entirely. If you are struggling, accept it, and let go of what you were trying to do. The universe is trying to tell you that particular relationship, job, school, etc is not good for you and will take you off of your path.

Ultimately, if you continue to struggle and continue to insist, the universe may eventually, begrudgingly deliver; and it will set you up to learn some hard lessons.

People, places, things, experiences, etc that lead you to your purpose will come "easily" (that does not mean quickly or with zero effort... but it will not feel like struggle). Be mindful of what you are asking for, and WHY you are asking for it. Recognize struggle, and act on it, and you will get to your purpose and a fulfilling life much faster.

If you are struggling, accept it, and let go of what you were trying to do. The universe is trying to tell you that particular relationship, job, school, etc is not good for you and will take you off of your path.

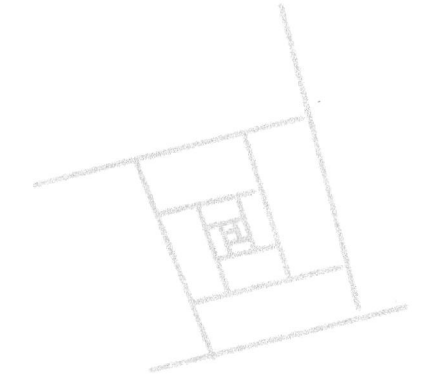

Stage Three: I Am My Needs

Not sorry
I have needs
You'll just have to
Take second seat
It's about me
But about me
I need
I spin in my
Self-center
Vacant void
Missing something
I can't quite explain
Restrained
Voice vacant
Void of all but
My own
Human nature

Characteristics

- Focused on what you perceive as your needs: food, sleep, attention, sex, money, etc.
- Other people are not individuals with needs but reflexes you can bring to bear to fulfill your own needs.
- Religion is learned through stories, experiences, images and people. Sense is made of religion based on how it can help fulfill your needs; what it can do for you.

Challenges

This is a very self-focused stage where you need to defend and fulfill your needs. However, it can be a stage where others are neglected as the collateral damage of your self-focused efforts. This can lead to alienating friends and family. It can turn you into a self-centered jerk that no one wants to be around. You must find a way to balance the fulfillment of your needs without using others and without disregarding the fact that they have needs too. This stage is very common in children and some young adults. Crisis, injury, surgery, and other medical issues will easily draw you back to this stage at any age. Because it is so self-focused, this stage is a great time to start examining your baggage from past relationships and childhood as well as an ideal stage to get out of debt (or at least start that process).

TASKS

☐ **Connect to your sexuality.**

☐ **Connect to the humanity of others** through their needs.

☐ **Connect with yourself** beyond your needs.

☐ As you realize that you are not your needs, but you HAVE needs, don't forget that you still need to attend to your needs. Although they are not you, if you do not attend to them, you can easily fall into spending extra time in this stage.

☐ **Connect with your internal energy and feelings.**

☐ **Connect with your money** - eliminate the chains of debt servitude from your life.

> ### Resources
>
> - *How to Win Friends and Influence People* by Dale Carnegie
> - *Total Money Makeover* by Dave Ramsey
> - *Love, Sex and Awakening* by Margot Anand

Questions To Fuel Your Thinking

- Are you nothing but your need for food, etc? Are you nothing but your need for sex? Do you have something else to offer this world?

- If you are not your needs, what are you?

- What are you feeling?

- What baggage do you have from childhood?

- What limiting beliefs did you pick up from your parents that may be wrong for you?

- What baggage do you have from past relationships?

- What limiting beliefs did you pick up along the way that may need to be replaced?

- What is your baggage signal? How do you know when you have just triggered your baggage? (Yelling, anger, crying, shutting down, something else?)

Connecting To Your Sexuality - Mind, Body And Energy

Connecting to your sexuality is about body and mind and energy all at the same time. Because it is not just about your body, let's start with the mind.

What are your current beliefs about your sexuality and sexuality in general?

What societal beliefs did you grow up with?

Do you agree with those?

What past experiences have you had?

What did they teach you?

Do you think those lessons are true?

Lastly, what are your current needs in this area?

Connecting to your sexuality is about body and mind and energy all at the same time.

Your sexual needs might include things like safety, trust, a healthy regular partner, more frequency, less frequency or specific types of exploration. You may have past trauma that you need to let go of. Or you might need to take a break from sexuality for a while. That is OK too. As always, **be honest with yourself.**

Few subjects can bring up feelings of guilt, shame, unworthiness and inadequacy like sexuality. It is rare to get to adulthood and NOT have some feelings or issues to work out in this area. Look to not just your experiences but even your childhood for clues as to why you feel that way.

Catalog your beliefs.

Understand your needs.

Explore your energy.

Breathe, pause, breathe.

How were you raised?

What lessons did your parents inadvertently teach you just by the way they treated each other?

Understand WHY you feel the way you do and have compassion for yourself as human.

Sexuality can be a powerful catalyst for connecting to the energy in your body. Many people will say that they cannot feel energy in their body. However, sexual energy is energy too. The next time your are enjoying your sexuality, alone or with another, place your attention on the feelings in your body. Feel the energy rise and move up from your root chakra.

Breathe deeply and slowly and imagine the energy flowing down and out when you exhale and up and higher when you inhale. Take a pause at the top and bottom of each breath and see what happens then.

Sexuality, in its most positive forms, is about a merging of body, mind and energy in a way that can connect us more deeply to ourselves and our partner. In this way, sexuality can also help you connect to others, to see their humanity and their needs.

Encourage your partner to explore their own sexuality in this way. If you can provide a safe and trusted place where you can both be open and honest, you will be amazed at the result. Connections will deepen and your reward will be more exciting and fulfilling experiences both in and out of the bedroom.

Connecting To Yourself - You Are More Than Your Needs And Wants

In the last stage (Stage Two), you focused on listing your needs and making sure they are met. The importance of meeting your needs has not changed just because you have evolved. However, it is time to understand your connection to those needs in more detail. Some things are true needs: food, clothing, shelter, safety, sleep, and the categories that you worked with in Stage Two. Sometimes you may convince yourself that you need something else: a new gadget, car, job, partner, etc.

When you feel that you NEED something, ask yourself why. Keep asking why until you get to the truth (usually at least five times). The truth is that you think you need it because it will make you FEEL a certain way.

For example, maybe you think you need a new car. Why? Is your old one broken down and cannot be fixed for what it is worth? You are worried about getting to work. A new car would make you feel safe. Or is your current car just fine but this new car will make you feel successful? Will it help you forget about your debt? Because you think maybe then you will finally have the attention of the women or men you desire? Because you ultimately feel unworthy and incomplete? Are you expecting this car to make you whole? Are you expecting it to make you feel worthy of the love and respect that you withhold from yourself? Is this car part of a persona you are trying to project? **Be brutally honest with yourself**.

Once you know the truth of why you think you need something, it is easy to be honest with yourself that you simply want it and to understand why.

What do you have to offer this world? Beyond your needs; beyond your wants?

Consider the idea that **you HAVE needs and wants, but they are not you.** You need sleep, but you are more than your need for sleep. You need food, sex, human connection, income, and many other things. But you are more than your need for food. You are more than your need for human connection. What do you have to offer this world? Beyond your needs; beyond your wants?

As you realize that you are not your needs, but you HAVE needs, don't forget that you still need to attend to your needs. Although they are not you, if you do not attend to them, you can easily fall into spending extra time in this stage.

When you feel that you NEED something, ask yourself why. Keep asking why until you get to the truth (usually at least five times). The truth is that you think you need it because it will make you FEEL a certain way.

Connecting To Others - Seeing Their Humanity Through Their Needs

When in stage three (I am my needs), the best way to move out of this stage and into Stage Four is to learn to see the humanity of others, through their needs. Try this exercise:

Choose someone you care about and a situation they are dealing with right now ...

1. **How would YOU feel in that situation?**

2. **What would you need?**

3. **Can you provide that for them even just a little?**

4. **Do it!**

5. **Then note how you feel.**

You will find that it does not take much to make a big impact. If someone is down, they might need a friend. Even a phone call may do. If someone is sick, you could bring them some food or help clean up the house or just sit with them for a bit.

The point is to get outside of your head and beyond your needs and explore the needs of others. When you put yourself in their situation and feel what it must be like to be them, it becomes easier to see their humanity. It becomes easier to see how they are not so different from you, and you can help. Once you help a little, you are likely to help more.

The point is to get started with those you hold most dear. When you are ready, try the same exercise with people you do not know, but have heard about. Work your way out to asking these questions about people you do not like at all. You might not go so far as to help, but just putting yourself in their shoes will help you see their humanity and that will make all the difference.

It does not take much to make a big impact.

Connecting To Your Internal Energy And Feelings

Everyone has feelings. Sometimes you feel sad, or happy, or stressed, or overwhelmed. Feelings are how your body, mind and intuition guide you to make better choices. Connecting to your feelings means stopping to recognize them and explore what is causing them. **It does not mean that you need to express every feeling you have out loud.** You can keep your feelings to yourself if you want to, or share them, if appropriate. The important thing is to step back from your emotions, name them, and dig deeper to find the real cause.

Step back from your emotions, name them, and dig deeper to find the real cause.

For example, suppose you find yourself angry at your spouse. It is a good idea to take a moment. Stop. Breathe. Ask yourself why you are angry. You will likely tell yourself a story about what they did that made you angry. Next, ask yourself what you are afraid of. All anger is rooted in fear. What are you afraid of? You might be afraid that you are not important. You might be afraid that you are not useful or needed. Be brutally honest with yourself. When you can, you might express to your spouse that, "when you do X, I fear that I am not important to you." (fill in the right actions and fears). Being honest about what you feel, and more importantly why you feel it, is critical to a connected relationship.

When you are disconnected from your feelings, your feelings will control you. **If you would rather be in control of your feelings, you will need to connect with them, not ignore them.** you will need to sit down with your emotions and really understand them. This becomes faster with practice.

Many emotions are rooted in validating our current definition of self. We want to define ourselves as important and we fear that we are wrong. Fear, in particular, is often associated with something counter to our definition of self. We fear, at the root of it all, that our definition of self is wrong; that who we think we are, is not true. This fear of being wrong about ourselves leads to a defensive anger. Can you see how there are layers to your emotions? Digging deeper reveals the truth. Shining a light on the truth makes it dissipate.

Fear of being wrong about ourselves leads to a defensive anger.

These feelings are trying to tell you something. Just like your gut instinct or intuition is often trying to tell you something you need to know. Similarly, your energy is trying to tell you something. Some people find connecting to their energy hard to do. Initially, you may not feel energy in your body. That is OK.

Everything in the universe is made of matter and energy. Think about your phone or computer. It has a screen but it also has electrical energy running through it that makes it work. Without the electricity, it would be lifeless. So would you. You have energy running through you too. Without it, you would be lifeless too. Connecting to your energy is the first step in recognizing a vast amount of information available to you about your body, your life and many other things. Connecting to your energy at this stage means learning to recognize it and be aware of how it changes.

Emotions move your energy. Think about when you feel really happy. There is a feeling in your chest like your heart is full. That is, you heart is full of energy! Think about when you feel nervous or fearful. There is a feeling in your stomach. Your emotions are moving the energies in your gut to get your attention.

On a sexual note, think about the feeling of an orgasm (solo or with someone else). You might feel a burst of energy that moves up and through you. Either way, it feels like release. It is a release of energy.

Emotions move your energy.

So you can see that you have been feeling your energies all along. To connect to them with more awareness, try the following…

Scan your body for feelings and for energy. Where is energy moving? What are you feeling there? What is the truth it is trying to tell you? Listen without bias.

Body Scanning - sit, quiet your mind, and scan your body from the top down, or from the bottom up. Just think about each part of your body and how your body feels. Do you have some tension in the muscles, or maybe some pain from an injury? Notice that when you put your awareness on a tense muscle, it tends to relax. As with all things in this life, shining a spotlight on the problem makes it dissolve away, or makes a solution apparent. For areas or your body that are not tense or in pain, ask yourself what they feel like. You may notice small sensations that grow as you focus on them. This is your energy. You may feel it more in one area than another. That is OK. You may notice that you feel it more in specific locations up the front of your body. These are your chakras. For now, just explore and sit for a minute with what you find.

Reiki / Energy Work - When body scanning is not enough, or you just want to try something new, you might accelerate your connection to your energy by enjoying a session of Reiki or other energy work. It is important that your first experience be hands-on. Some energy practitioners are adept at sending energy from a distance but you may not feel it if you are not yet connected to your energy. Hands-on techniques are much more effective for sparking your awareness of your energy. This might look like a massage session that includes energy work, or a session that focuses on energy work, such as Reiki. Be open to the experience and let it show you that there is so much more out there to explore and understand about yourself and this existence.

Once you connect to your energy, you might forget about your feelings. Try to remain aware of both. **For a while, include body scanning in your mediation/prayer practice to improve your connection to both your feelings and your energy.** See where it takes you.

Connecting To Your Money - Getting Out Of Debt

Connecting to your money means keeping careful watch on what is coming in and what is going out. It means consciously directing your money to act in your best interests. **Consider your beliefs about money that may need to be updated.** Are they serving you? What new beliefs do you need to put in place? You have a relationship with money whether you want one or not. Make friends with your money, do the right things with your money, and more money will come to you in ways you may not currently imagine.

Connecting to your money means keeping careful watch on what is coming in and what is going out. It means consciously directing your money to act in your best interests.

Credit card debt, student loans, car loans, personal loans and the like are all forms of servitude. You are a slave, working for the bank or family member that lent you the money. Your time and effort belong to them, not you. This should be terrifying. In many cultures around the world, debt is considered normal. We are taught that debt is a tool for building assets and wealth. Debt is a tool in one way. It is a tool for banks and others to keep you under control and to keep your hard earned money coming to them instead of you. If you are not currently in debt, that is great! Stay that way.

If you are currently in debt, through student loans, car loans, credit cards, personal loans, payment plans for things you bought, or anything else, getting out of debt needs to be a major priority. **Being debt-free will be the foundation of creating an amazing stress-free life.** Imagine what you could do if you did not have debt payments? What could you do with that money instead?

You could save for your dreams and make them happen. You could take that class, or write that book or live that lifestyle that you have been dreaming of. You could save up to be financially independent - that is, you could save and invest to the point that you did not need to work at all. Your dreams and purpose and joy could be your work.

Debt = Servitude

Dave Ramsey's baby steps and debt snowball are a tried and true method for this…

First, make a list of every debt you have. Include everything: credit cards, car loans, student loans, money you owe friends and family and other individuals, payment plans you have on things you bought, your home mortgage, etc. It may seem overwhelming. That is OK. Let the weight of your reality settle on you. Acknowledge the fear and the overwhelm. This too is being human. Then say…

OK. THIS has got to go. Set your determination and make it solid. This ends today. No more new debt, EVER.

Order your debts from smallest to largest. This is the order you will use to pay them off. Why? Because it builds momentum, physiological advantage and continually adds more money to your efforts over time.

Next, **make a list of all the money you have** in any account (savings, checking, investments, etc). What do you have that you can put towards paying off this debt? Do it today. It will be painful at first to see your savings go towards this debt but this is an important first step.

Keep for yourself, or save up, a small **emergency fund** that is large enough to cover a major car repair or home repair. This will prevent emergencies from taking you off track.

Then, **make a budget**. Call it a spend plan if that feels better. But list out your expenses and your income. **Cut your expenses to the core.** There are likely many things you can do without, just for a while, as you pay off your debts. Get creative. The key is sticking to your spend plan ruthlessly and paying off your debts one by one. You will be amazed at the momentum and positive energy you will feel as you carry this out. As each debt is paid off, and you no longer have that payment to make each month, there is more money you can put on next debt. Read about the baby steps on Dave Ramsey's website. Listen to his shows and podcasts for inspiration and to help keep you on track.

Know where your money is.

Direct it where to go.

Make a new budget every month and stick to it.

Stage Four: Others Have Needs Too
(I Am My Needs And Others Are Their Needs)

*Suddenly populated
These people I
Long predated
Pre-dated
Have they always been here?
Pious I
Righteous in my
Newfound awareness
Here and now isn't
It enough to help
Martyr myself
To be better than them
Pious I
Am split
Above and below*

Characteristics

- You see others as individuals with needs of their own; it is not their job to fulfill your needs.
- You practice prioritizing your needs above or below others, and others above or below each other.
- Conscience, guilt, shame, and empathy are now possible and even likely (but can also be faked).
- Your deity is seen as a personified, anthropomorphic, named being who is focused on justice.
- You take religious metaphors, stories and symbolism literally.

Challenges

Although this stage is far less self-centered, it is still focused on your own needs. Financial strain, work stress and other situations that cause scarcity can pull you back to this stage. Fear of loss reigns supreme along with the fear of not having your needs met. There can be a lot of guilt, regret and shame in this stage when reflecting on your past actions. If there are people you need to apologize to, this is a good time to do it.

TASKS

☐ **Connect to others** - find ways to help others fulfill their needs.

Connect to yourself...

☐ Attend to your needs.

☐ Reflect on your past when you find patterns affecting you today.

☐ Define your value set / beliefs / ideologies and put it into practice.

Connect to your money...

☐ Solidify your savings engine.

☐ If you are not yet out of debt, double down on your efforts.

☐ If you are debt free (good job!), think about the funds you will need in the future and save, save, save.

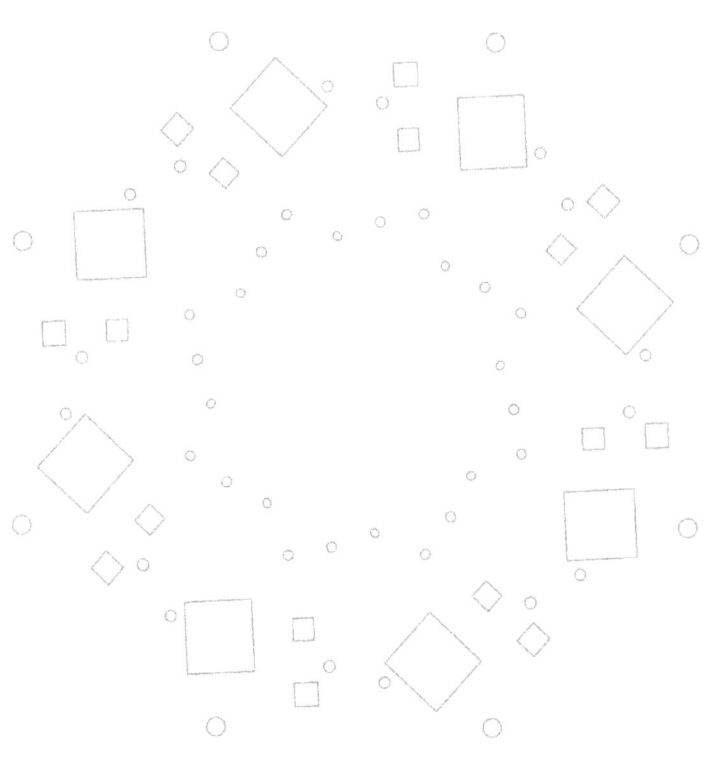

> ### Resources
>
> - Your religious text(s) of choice
> - *Principles* by Ray Dalio
> - *The Jordan Harbinger Show* Podcast
> - Writings and speeches by His Holiness The Dalai Lama

Questions To Fuel Your Thinking

- Are their situations when you used others to fulfill your own needs, without regard to theirs? How would you handle those situations differently?

- What are you feeling?

- Who do you need to apologize to? Can you reach out to them?

- Can you let go of your past now and move forward?

- How do you currently prioritize your needs over or under the needs of others? Would you like to change that in order to find balance? Do you prioritize others too much above yourself? Or do you prioritize yourself too much above others? What should your principles be for prioritizing your needs and the needs of those you care about?

- What, according to your religion or other sources, should be the guiding principles of your life? Do you agree with those? How would you edit them for YOUR life?

Connecting To Yourself And Others - Attending To Needs As Part Of A Regular Routine

Now that you can imagine the needs of others, it is time to make helping others a part of your regular routine. This could be as simple as regular coffee with your friends, where you take stock of what they need emotionally and support them in that way. It could be volunteering regularly at your favorite charity. It could be something completely new. If there is a particular group of people (veterans, homeless, children, etc) that you feel drawn to help, think about unique ways that you can help, that may not be covered by anyone else. The key is to make and maintain a regular routine of caring for the needs of others in a way that takes advantage of your unique perspective and gifts. Be careful not to fall into the trap of just giving money. **Give your time, effort and creativity.** Be there in person with the people you are helping, if possible. Connect to them in that space.

Make and maintain a regular routine of caring for the needs of others in a way that takes advantage of your unique perspective and gifts.

While attending to the needs of others is important, attending to your own needs is more important. Creating a routine for attending to your needs is a great way to make sure you do not neglect them. As humans, we have so many needs: mental, emotional, physical, spiritual, intellectual, etc. It can seem overwhelming. Routines make it simple and easy to ensure that your needs are being met.

This body, mind and spirit must be maintained and sacred routines are one way to make sure that happens.

From previous effort, you should have a list of your needs in order of the following categories... something like this:

- Physical Needs - sleep, regeneration, exercise, sex, nutrition, hygiene
- Mental/Emotional Needs - intellectual activities, relationships, time alone
- Spiritual Needs - prayer/meditation, study, rituals, services, retreats, etc
- Medical Needs - services, doctor visits, etc
- Professional or Purpose-Driven Needs - training, knowledge, action

Now map these needs into real action on your daily or weekly calendar. Schedule in time for sleep, regenerative activities, time for exercise, eating well, hygiene and even sex. Schedule time for relationships, prayer/meditation, and everything else. You may find that there are optimal times of day for specific tasks. For example, if you are a morning person, you might find that language learning followed by mediation and then exercise makes a nice routine. The optimal routine is different for everyone. **Experiment to find your best fit.** Then, schedule it and hold it sacred.

If you do not make your needs a priority, nobody else will, and you will become unable to help anyone else. Being a martyr is not good for you and ultimately makes you unable to pursue your purpose. This body, mind and spirit must be maintained and sacred routines are one way to make sure that happens.

What routines will you experiment with? What order of things might be best for you?

Connecting To Yourself - Recognizing And Removing Negative Patterns

Humans are creatures of pattern. We fall into routines easily. Our behavior is no different. Some behavioral patterns are good for you. Consistently working out or consistently learning something new results in good things. However, If there are negative patterns in your behavior - if you do the same thing over and over in a way that hurts you, now is the time to recognize that and remove the root cause. Negative patterns can take many forms in many areas of you life, from finance to relationships, physical or health issues, parenting and more.

Step one is to recognize the negative pattern. Do you already know what it is? For example, is food what you turn to when you are stressed? Do you overspend your budget in certain areas? Do you not buckle your seatbelt and therefore put yourself at risk? Do you find yourself with abusive partners over and over? Do you cause your own demise at work, job after job? When something negative happens in your life, examine if this is the first time. Or does it seem to happen all the time? If it is a pattern, acknowledge that. If it is a one-time thing, acknowledge that too.

Next, examine the cause. The root of the behavior is often buried below layers of psychological excuses. You will have to dig to find it.

Why, Why, Why? ...

One great way to do that is to ask yourself the question, "Why?", and to keep asking why until you reach the root cause. For example, the progression might look like this: why do I eat when I am stressed? Because it makes me feel better. Why? because it makes me feel cared for. Why does it make me feel cared for? Because my parents always would give me food when I was upset as a way to quiet me down. AHA! Now we have it. There was a pattern established in childhood that put the belief in your head that food is how we calm down. Cookies became the security blanket of anything stressful or upsetting. But now this pattern is harming your health, your self image, your opportunities, and so much more. But by shining a light on the truth, you will find that it dissipates. Now that you know the root cause, you can see that you need a mechanism to comfort yourself in times of stress. If you recognize how the pattern started, you can establish an alternate method of comforting yourself and slowly the urge to eat when you are stressed will go away.

Tony Robbins's Parent-Centered Approach...

Another method that works wonders comes from Tony Robbins. In this method, you consider the question: which of your parent's love did you crave the most? You surely wanted love and acceptance from both but there was one that you wanted it from MORE. Which parent was that? Then, what did you have to BE to get that love and acceptance?

Negative Emotions As The Root Of Patterns...

Sometimes a negative emotion is the root of your pattern. Practice recognizing and naming your feelings. For example, you may give your children too much for too long, ultimately harming their ability to create independence, all because you feel guilt about what they went through in the past.

When feeling guilt, shame, regret, sadness, or other negative emotions, ask yourself why you feel this way. Take the time to explore your reactions (do not suppress them). Keep asking why you feel this way until you get to the real root of the issue. Acknowledge your truth and remind yourself that it is all part of being human.

When negative emotions are fertilizing the roots of your harmful patterns, it is important to be compassionate to yourself. Regret, in particular, requires a lot of self compassion to heal. Remind yourself that you did what you could at the time given who you were and the circumstances that surrounded you. You are a different person now. Can you imagine sitting with that old version of yourself and offering compassion like a good friend? Work to let these feelings go, by shining a spotlight on them every time they appear, and offering compassion to yourself and anyone else involved. In time, these feelings will dissolve along with the patterns they cause.

Lastly, as you recognize unhealthy patterns, you will need to either replace them with healthy patterns or stop them cold. Rules help. Make a list of rules to operate by. It helps to have rules to remind yourself what to do in specific situations. **What rules do you need to put in place to avoid falling into negative patterns?**

Recognize the pattern.

Dig for the cause.

Replace or stop the pattern.

Connecting To Your Ideology - Define Your ideology And Put It Into Practice

Your ideology is nothing more than a set of values, rules, beliefs and ideas that you use to make decisions. Every decision you make, if not based on emotion or subconscious beliefs, is ultimately based on your ideology. Your ideology can be a very emotional thing and it might be hard to distinguish between an ideological or an emotional root for your choices. It is OK for emotions and ideology to mix for now. At this point, the task is to focus on defining your ideology and putting it into practice in your life.

Try the following...

First, **write down what you want your beliefs or values to be** in these areas ...

- Religion
- Politics
- Social / moral issues
- How you should treat others
- Food and nutrition
- Health and wellbeing
- Anything and everything else

Your list will start to get pretty long but just keep going. Even if it takes weeks to get your list together, it is worth it. Write it all down.

Next, **ask yourself why you want these particular beliefs**. Is it because other people (parents, friends, etc) have suggested (overtly or through their behavior) that these are what your beliefs should be? Is it because of your experiences? Is it to avoid negative consequences? What consequences are you trying to avoid?

Be honest about what you truly believe at this moment and why you believe it. Examine if you think those beliefs need to change or be updated in some way?

When you have your list, understand why you believe each item, and have made updates, it is time to **aggregate them to the level of PRINCIPLES**. Principles are not issue-specific. Principles are meta-beliefs. They are the reason behind several beliefs. For example, your beliefs might include that credit cards are evil and car loans are a bad idea and payment plans are also a bad idea. The principle behind all of these is that debt in any form is a bad idea; or you might say that the principle is that debt is slavery and you don't want to be a slave. That is really two principles there... Debt is slavery... and I will not be a slave. The principle of, "I will not be a slave," might have have spawned many other beliefs in your ideology all by itself. Principles are the root of beliefs.

Are there underlying principles that are common to your beliefs? What principles are the overarching guides? Could you use principles for your ideology instead of specific rules/beliefs?

Principles give you a more general framework for making decisions and a shorter list of items in your ideology. Dozens of beliefs and rules might boil down to just a small number of principles. Principles also play another critical role - they highlight our inconsistencies and hypocrisy.

Are some of your beliefs in contradiction to your principles? List your beliefs in one column and your principles in another. Do you have any principles that are in conflict with each other? Do you have any beliefs that are in conflict with one of your principles? How can you update your principles and beliefs to **eliminate contradictions and inconsistencies**? Lastly, can you put your principles in **priority order**? Are some more important than others? At the end of all of these exercises, you should have a comprehensive list of your principals, in priority order, that you can use to make better decisions at your job, in the voting booth, at the grocery and everywhere else.

Understand that your ideology will evolve with you and that is a good thing. Be ready to update your ideology as you learn and experience new things and perspectives.

List your beliefs.

Understand where they came from.

Update them as needed.

Aggregate them into principles.

Look for inconsistencies.

Adjust your principles and beliefs as needed.

Understand it will evolve over time.

Connecting To Your Money - Solidifying Your Savings Engine

In Stage Three, you made some very important things: a list of all your debts, a plan to pay them off and a spend plan or budget that would make the whole thing work. **This spend plan, and your ability to stick to it, is your SAVINGS ENGINE.** It is time to solidify it for the long term.

First, if you are not yet out of debt (that can take time), increase your efforts. Get a second or third job, cut back further on your expenses, sell everything, and do what you need to do to put more towards your debts. Run, do not walk, out of debt as if your life depends on it - because it does.

Second, if you are debt free (good job!), it is time to think about the funds you will need in the future and save, save, save. Only you can define your goals, but here are some examples…

- Going back to school for a degree
- Having children
- Becoming financially independent
- Putting kids through college
- Remodeling your home
- Buying a home or second home
- Paying off your mortgage
- Moving to another city or state or country
- Buying a car or new piece of technology
- Retiring early
- Traveling the world
- … get creative!

You are sure to have near term goals and long term goals. Goals should be reasonable, in the sense of being achievable in this lifetime. That being said, do not dismiss an idea just because the only way you know how to do it is too expensive. Get creative. Find ways that cost less. You can make your goals very reasonable and very achievable.

For example, you may want to save up to send your kids to college. Do they need an expensive out of state school? Probably not. Do you need to pay for ALL of it? No. Decide how much you will pay and be very specific. For example, if you have many children and cannot realistically pay for four years for all of them, you might offer to pay for two years for each of them, being very specific about what those two years will include. This is just one example. Understand that your goals may not look like anyone else's and that is OK.

Keep a list of your goals where you can see them every day. Keeping track of your goals makes you less likely to sabotage your progress.

The savings engine - your monthly spend plan that includes consistently putting money towards debt and then towards goals - is the key to achieving any goal you can define. If you can consistently save a minimum amount per month, then you will eventually meet your goals. Consistency is they key. Your savings engine (or debt payment engine) should be a critical line item in your monthly spend plan - a number that you track and report to yourself each month. How much did you put towards debt or save up for your goals? Can you do more? As the saying goes, "What gets measured, gets managed." So measure your progress. You will find yourself automatically pushing harder to do more.

Consider prioritizing your goals based on what will happen first, or what is most important, and tackle them one at a time, just like you did for paying off debt. Dave Ramsey's baby steps recommend that saving a 4-6 month emergency fund, and then saving for children's college and retirement should be important enough to be at the very top of the list. You are sure to have other goals beyond those.

Investments may help you put your savings engine in overdrive. Although investments are not without significant risk, over the long term, they can be a powerful component of your savings engine. When saving for retirement and other goals that are at least 5 years away, consider working with an investment manager, or getting smart on investments yourself, to make your money work harder. Compound interest is the key to major long term wealth and financial independence. A good financial manager, or your company's retirement plan administrator, can help you send money directly into a retirement account from your paychecks as part of your dedicated savings engine. Read up on Dave Ramsey's methods and recommendations for more ideas and advice.

Consistency is key.

Save. Save. Save.

Do not dismiss a goal just because you think it is too expensive - find a more creative way.

Stage Five: I Am My Value Set / Ideology / Religion / Beliefs

*Look
I can't keep
Martyring
Bartering for priority
It's not me
Harsh ruler
It is ideology
Determines
You are lesser
Or equal
In my infinite wisdom
Thank god you have me
To show you the way*

Characteristics

- You define yourself based on a set of social, moral, political and religious values.
- You have a strong affinity for laws and ethical codes.
- Anything that conflicts with your ideology is ignored or attacked.
- When you see or hear something that conflicts with your ideology, you feel offended or angry.
- You see people with other ideologies as lesser or lower than you, or not human at all, or deserving of bad things.

Challenges

This stage is very challenging because you feel offended and shocked more often than you feel anything else. And just when you think you are beyond this, there is nothing like a good election, news program or religious retreat to pull you back into your ideology. Reading headlines focused on defending and attacking ideologies (political, religious or otherwise) will keep you in this stage far longer than is necessary and will only exacerbate the negatives of this stage. While it is important to HAVE an ideology just to get through your day and make good choices, it is more important to avoid swinging it at everyone who may feel differently. The biggest challenge in this stage is to have and evolve an ideology but to keep it on the shelf instead of wearing it. Your ideology is there for reference, but you are so much more.

TASKS

Connect to yourself...

☐ Read about other ideologies - political, social, religious, etc.

☐ Resist the urge to attack or be rude to others who think differently than you. It may feel justified right now but will be yet one more thing you will have to forgive yourself for in later stages.

☐ Return to your principles... based on new experiences, do they need to be updated?

☐ Consider that you HAVE an ideology, but you are so much more.

☐ **Connect to others** - see their humanity through their ideology. (Understand that if they are also in this stage, they may attack or ignore you if you try to sway them. So do not try to sway them, or anyone else. You will be ignored, or attacked and will ultimately not sway anyone.)

Don't forget to:

☐ Stay connected to your body, movement, sexuality, health, energy and feelings.

☐ Stay connected to your money - resist debt in any form, maintain your savings engine and save for your dreams.

☐ Maintain your needs.

☐ Update your principles and ideology as new experiences shape you.

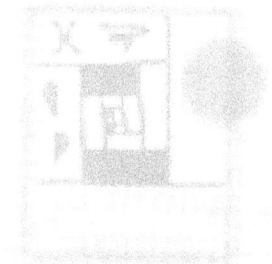

> **RESOURCES**
>
> - The political platforms of each major party in your country (yes, all of them) and those of other countries
> - Every religious text you can find (*The Bible, The Torah, The Qur'an, The Bhagavad Gita, The Tao Te Ching, The Dhammapada*, etc)
> - *The Four Agreements* by Don Miguel Ruiz

Questions To Fuel Your Thinking

- What aspects or big ideas or underlying truths from other religious texts, other political platforms and other ways of thinking do you connect with?

- Are there some changes you would like to make to update your own principles or ideologies?

- Could you reframe your ideology further around principles instead of specific issues?

- If you are not your ideology, not your needs, not your experiences…. what are you? Are you ready to maybe not know for a while?

Connecting To Yourself - Reading About Other Ideologies And Updating Your Own

Stage Five can be a very challenging stage. To complete it as completely as possible and move on to Stage Six as quickly as possible, you will have to get comfortable with other people's ideologies, as well as your own. You do not have to agree with them. But you do need to see why they might think that way. **The goal is to get to the point where you can have your ideology, but not feel offended when you hear a different one.** It takes practice.

Read about other ideologies - political, social, religious, etc - read it all from an anthropological viewpoint. The point of this reading is not to change your mind. The point is to become aware of the details of other ideologies…. to educate yourself about what other people believe. Just read to say, "isn't that interesting."

During your reading, and even during your daily life, you are sure to feel offended sometimes when your ideology is attacked, or when reading something counter to your beliefs. When you feel offended, step back from that feeling and recognize that you, as a human in this stage, are prone to feel offended when you encounter something that goes against your ideology because your ideology (at this point) IS you and your mind sees it as an attack on your very self. Detach from that feeling and note to yourself that this too is human. That will help it pass.

Eventually, you will not feel offended anymore. It is a liberating state to be in.

In your daily life and online life, you may to be tempted to lash out at those who think differently. Resist the urge to attack or be rude to others who think differently than you. It may feel justified right now, but will be yet one more thing you will have to forgive yourself for in later stages. You are not going to change their minds. All you will do is make yourself look like a jerk, setting a bad stereotype for your own ideology. A good rule is: If you don't have anything nice to say, don't say anything at all.

While it is important to spend a little time defining yourself by your ideology (the essence of Stage Five), it is best to try and shorten your time in this stage. There are so many negative emotions here and Stage Six, just one step away is so much more peaceful and joyous. Let's get there quickly.

Consider that you HAVE an ideology, but you are so much more. You have a lot more to offer this world than just your belief set. Just as you HAVE needs, but you are more than your needs, you HAVE an ideology (and psychologically must have an ideology), but you are so much more. Your needs are part of being human and your ideology helps you make better choices. But you are MORE than just these things. You have contributions to make to humanity; a purpose.

Now that you have a little distance and perspective on your ideology, and awareness of other ideologies, return to your principles… based on new experiences, do they need to be updated? How will your new principles alter your ideology on specific issues of religion, politics, social/moral issues, and how you might interact with others, yourself and the world?

Read about other ideologies.

Practice understanding why they might think that way.

If you don't have anything nice to say, don't say anything at all.

Update your principles as needed.

The answer might be that no updates are needed right now. That is OK. Or the answer might be that major updates are needed. That is OK too. Keep these questions at hand. Return to your principles regularly to evolve them as your experiences change your perspectives. Keeping them up to date will help you maintain this vital mechanism for better decisions in your own life. **There is not a single ideology that everyone arrives at.** There is no standard of moving from left to right or right to left.

We just evolve. Our needs evolve. Our ideologies evolve; and not always in the direction that everyone else might appear to move. This too is human. The key is to consciously evolve your ideology as life evolves you.

Connecting To Others - Seeing Their Humanity Through Their Ideology

Imagine someone you know that has a different opinion or ideology than you. Political ideologies are the most obvious candidates but it might be easier to start with someone who has a different religious ideology from you; or someone who simply prefers to dress differently than you would. Even someone who likes different foods. Preferably someone you like. Start easy because this is a really challenging exercise.

Do not try to sway them, or anyone else. That is not why we are here. Instead of trying to change their minds, put yourself in their shoes. This is not to change your mind either. **The point here is to simply examine their past and see why they might think that way.**

When you feel offended, angry or threatened at the thought of someone else's beliefs, what you are really feeling is fear. **Deep down in your subconscious, you fear that you are wrong, or that they will try to infringe on your way of life.** 99.999% of the time, despite the headlines stoking your fears, your fears are completely unwarranted. Put these feelings aside for just a little while and try this exercise.

Can you see how something in their current daily life, in their childhood or their past would make them think that way? Given how they grew up and what they have experienced, does it make sense that they might believe that?

Think of someone you disagree with.

Can you see why they might think the way they do?

Can you see how they are just human, trying to find their way?

Send them compassion for the journey you share.

For example, suppose that they like tattoos and you think that tattoos are bad. Is there something in their background that might draw them to it? Was their childhood overly restrictive? What about tattoos is the real attraction? Expressiveness? Freedom of spirit? See deeper than the fact that they believe differently. See WHY they believe differently.

Now let's take a political example. Perhaps you have a friend that believes that the government should regulate more, provide more, and be something of a parent to the citizens. If you are more of a rugged individualist, you may find the notion threatening. Look past your reactions. Step back and ask yourself what in their life might have led them to these beliefs.

Did they grow up having more than average provided for them by their parents or their government, or someone else, even blind luck? Can you see how this positive experience of parent or government or spouse as life long provider might shape them to believe that they cannot do for themselves, or that they need someone to provide for them or even that they simply like having someone else provide for them? Maybe they do not mind or do not notice the inherent control their providers have over them. **Not everyone desires the same thing.**

Now turn that around. Suppose your friend is the rugged individualist. Can you see why they might feel that way? Did they have to work hard for what they have? Did they witness others, even their own siblings, be given more than they were? Can you feel the unfairness and threat they must have felt? Can you see why they might have chosen to rely only on themselves after such a demonstration that even their parents would not provide what they needed.

Remember that it is about more than money. Our emotional and other needs influence this as well.

You can disagree with them and still see how they might come to believe what they believe. You can have your own beliefs and they can have theirs. Most importantly, they do not have to be wrong for you to be right. Their beliefs can be right for them right now and your beliefs can be right for you right now. When it comes to politics, religion, and simply how to live life, we all have our own beliefs, forged from parental influence and years of experiences. These beliefs, however, are just that - beliefs. They are more opinion than fact.

You can disagree with them and still see how they might come to believe what they believe. You can have your own beliefs and they can have theirs. Most importantly, they do not have to be wrong for you to be right.

I challenge you to repeat this exercise for as many people as you can think of: family, friends, coworkers, political figures, etc. **start with people you like and work your way up to people that you do not like at all.**

Feel their humanity and see that they are on the same path that you are. They are more than their beliefs. They are human like you. They have needs and a purpose (even if they don't know what it is yet). They are traversing this cycle of development just like you. Eventually, they will see your humanity too. Can you see theirs? **Close your eyes, think of them, and feel compassion for the fact that they are human too, trying to find their way.**

Keep in mind that some people you may think of in this exercise will be adults in stage three (I am my needs) and that makes them dangerous. You can feel compassion for their humanity and their journey without making yourself vulnerable to predators and other dangerous personalities. Compassion does not mean you need to have contact with them. **Compassion from a distance is still compassion** and in some cases is the healthiest approach. They key is to feel their humanity and offer compassion for their journey, quietly from within yourself.

Stage Six: To Each Their Own (I Am My Ideology And Others Are Theirs)

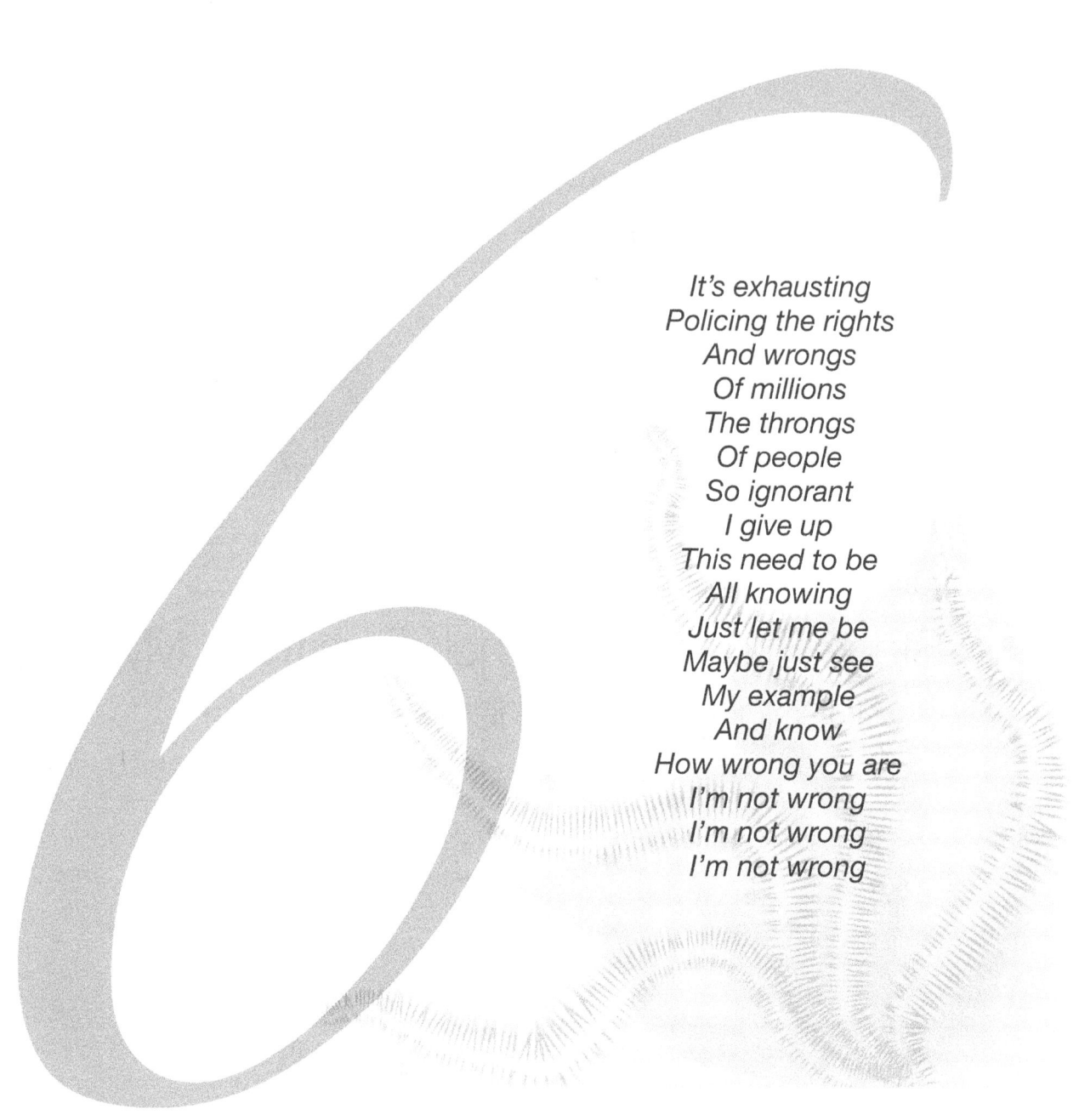

*It's exhausting
Policing the rights
And wrongs
Of millions
The throngs
Of people
So ignorant
I give up
This need to be
All knowing
Just let me be
Maybe just see
My example
And know
How wrong you are
I'm not wrong
I'm not wrong
I'm not wrong*

Characteristics

- You can put yourself in other people's shoes and feel what it is like to be them. You can see why they would have a different ideology and what that would be.
- You can consider other ideologies without feeling like yours is being attacked, and without attacking others.
- You reflect on the inconsistencies and complexities of your ideologies and are comfortable with them.
- ...But you think there might be something more; a larger perspective or truth that you are missing.

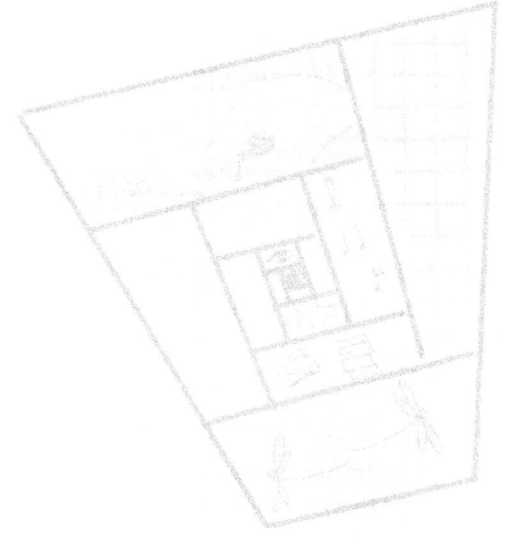

Challenges

There are far fewer challenges in this stage. You feel much happier with your life. Although you are still defined by your ideology, you are living in a bit of a fantasy world in thinking that your ideology is perfect, or that the inconsistencies are OK. Many adults stay very happily in this stage for life. The treadmill of work, sleep, work, sleep can be a lifelong endeavor and can feel purposeful if you have work that you love. If however, you, like most, feel that call to figure out the truth of your self and your life and to design a life of peace, joy, excitement, or anything else you want… Complete this stage and proceed to stage seven.

TASKS

Connect to yourself...

☐ Return to your own ideology: Detail the cracks, the inconsistencies, hypocrisies and conflicts.

☐ Look in the mirror and see the person causing 99% of all your problems.

☐ Forgive and accept yourself as human.

☐ **Connect to your body** - Set specific, measurable, and attainable goals with near term milestones.

☐ **Connect to your heart** - See that you are worthy of your own love and of the infinite love inside you.

Connect to others...

☐ See everyone as a reflection of some aspect of yourself.

☐ Connect to the divine light inside them.

☐ Forgive and accept others as human.

☐ Forgive and accept the existence of aspects of society that you previously rejected (groups of people, norms, standards, societal rules, etc).

Don't forget to:

☐ Stay connected to your body, movement, sexuality, health, energy and feelings.

☐ Stay connected to your money - resist debt in any form, maintain your savings engine and save for your dreams.

☐ Maintain your needs.

☐ Update your principles and ideology as new experiences shape you.

☐ Consider if you are ready to go on the journey that the next few steps entail.

☐ Do not proceed to Stage Seven until you have addressed forgiveness of yourself and others.

Resources

- *The Four Hour Body* by Tim Ferriss
- *Life Lessons* by Elisabeth Kubler-Ross, M.D. and David Kessler
- *Peaks and Valleys* by Spenser Johnson
- *Who Moved My Cheese* by Spencer Johnson
- *Walden* by Henry David Thoreau
- *Civil Disobedience* by Henry David Thoreau
- *Vagabonding* by Ralph Potts
- Speeches by KRS—One (search YouTube for videos uploaded by audiences)

Questions To Fuel Your Thinking

- List out the problems you currently face - how are you responsible for them? How can you take responsibility for changing them?

- What do you need to forgive yourself for?

- What do you need to forgive others for?

- What is it to forgive?

- How much money can you save up and how fast?

- What is it to feel worthy of your own love?

- What is it to connect with others on all levels - intellectual, heart, soul, truth, energy?

Connecting To Yourself - Taking Responsibility For Your Life

One of the most critical things you can do is to take responsibility for your life. The following exercise is challenging, but well worth it. Find a mirror. Look into it. Look in the mirror and see the person causing 99% of all your problems. It was YOU who chose to get into those bad relationships. It was YOU who spent money you did not have. It was YOU who chose to take that job or leave that job... you get the idea.

> *Look in the mirror and see the person causing 99% of all your problems.*

Sometimes, very rarely, our problems are caused by someone else. But even in these very rare circumstances, you are the one ultimately responsible for solving it. **If you want to see change in your life, you will have to be the one to make it happen.** Stop blaming your challenges on anyone else - they were not likely the cause and they are certainly not the solution. This starts with recognizing your own role and your own authority.

You are the decision maker in your life. Ultimately, your choices determine your fate. You might feel forced into a choice. But the reality is, **even with a gun to your head, you have a choice.** Are you blaming others for your choices? Are you blaming others for your circumstances? That is one way to ensure your situation will never change.

It is time to take full responsibility and authority over your life. Your failures are yours. Your successes are yours. Your bad decisions, good decisions, internal self talk, plans and task lists are yours. Your time and attention are yours. **What will you do with that kind of authority?** What will you change and what will you keep the same?

Consider each area of your life: health, finance, relationships, professional life, etc. Examine your situation. Decide how you want it to be. Ignore societal rules. Ignore what everyone else thinks. Ignore the media. **What do YOU want?** Once you stop blaming others for what is wrong with your life, you can take that authority for yourself and make your life whatever you want it to be. For now, it is enough to simply stop blaming others, see your own role in your problems, and see your own authority to change it. You can make a plan and make it happen. Start making changes TODAY.

Connecting To Your Body - Setting Goals And Making Progress

In previous stages you chose a form of movement that you enjoy and that you can do every day or just most days. Movement connects you to your body and the wonderful things it is capable of. Now it is time to connect more deeply with your body by setting some goals and making progress towards them.

This does not have to be high pressure. In fact, goals that require too much too fast are a recipe for disappointment and setbacks. Try the following.... consider your nutrition, your exercise or movement, and your overall physical wellbeing. Make one goal for each of these.

It does not matter what the goal is, or what change in your eating habits you decide to try or what type of exercise you like best. Taking consistent action towards these goals will give you physical peace.

Taking consistent action towards these goals will give you physical peace.

Goals should be specific, measurable, and attainable with near term milestones. Break your goals down to something you can target each week and day. Here are some examples...

Nutrition

- Drink less caffeine. Current - four cups of coffee per day. Goal - two cups of coffee per day. Plan - drop down to three cups immediately, and then two cups next week.

- Eat more vegetables. Current - none. Goal - three servings per day. Plan - buy baby carrots and put them in my lunch immediately, add a salad to dinner by next week, and look up recipes for vegetable soups and breakfast ideas to try by the end of the month.

Exercise / Movement

- Run faster. Current - one mile in 15 minutes. Goal - one mile in 8 minutes. Plan - beat my old time by at least a few seconds each time I run.

- Walk more. Current - one mile per day. Goal - five miles per day. Plan - add a quarter mile per day until I reach five.

Overall Physical Wellbeing

- Get more sleep. Current - 6 hours per night average. Goal - 8 hours per night average. Plan - start bedtime routines and get to sleep 30 minutes earlier this week, then 30 minutes earlier again next week.... until 8 hours per night is the average.

These are just examples. They demonstrate how goals can start out general, but have a specific, measurable end and an incremental plan for meeting it. Deep down, you know what changes you need to make, so trust your gut. If you decide to have a larger, long term goal, that is OK. Make sure it has weekly success metrics to keep you motivated all the same. Daily is even better. What can you do today?

Most importantly, and this goes for ANY goal, your definition of success must not require someone else to do something. Your definition of success must be something that YOU can control.

You will find that making progress towards your own personally defined goals is addictive in the most wonderful way. When you feel like adding another goal, do It! As long as your goals are specific, measurable and attainable, with weekly and daily checks for progress, you are sure to achieve it.

If you are new to setting your own goals for your body, start small. Exercising your authority over your body and your life strengthens your ability to do even more later, if you want to. It is the key to optimizing your life. If you need accountability, tell a friend about your goals and have them ask you regularly about your progress, or find a friend who has the same goals. Another creative solution for motivation is to bet money on yourself that, if you fail, will be sent to some cause that makes you cringe. Motivation is very individual. Experiment to find out what works best for you.

Lastly, celebrate your successes, no matter how small you might think they are. Celebrate meeting your daily goals with positive self talk. Celebrate meeting your weekly goals with a treat of some kind. And celebrate your big long term goals with an equally big reward.

Ready? Set? Go!

Have a specific, measurable goal and an incremental plan for achieving it.

Connecting To Yourself - Forgiving And Accepting Yourself As Human

As you take responsibility for your life and authority for your future, you may find that you blame yourself too much. Taking responsibility for your circumstances is important. But continually beating yourself up over past regrets is entirely counterproductive. **It is time to forgive yourself and accept yourself as human.**

Think back to the experiences that you regret. Feel the regret. You may feel shame or disappointment as well. Let it come. **Lean into these feelings. This too is human.** This regret is leftover from a hard lesson. Hard lessons change you. Can you see yourself as a separate person from the one you are today? An earlier version of yourself? You are not the same. And you will not make that mistake again.

Taking responsibility for your circumstances is important. But continually beating yourself up over past regrets is entirely counterproductive.

Can you **see your humanity** and why, at that time in that situation, you chose to take those actions? Can you imagine sitting with yourself, feeling compassion for that version of yourself and telling yourself that you understand and feel their pain? Can you let that version of yourself go? You are not that person anymore and have learned from your experiences.

You are human just like everyone - we all make mistakes and have regrets. It is easy to see others as perfect people who have not made any mistakes. But that is not true. Everyone has regrets from hard lessons learned. They just hide it. If you learned from it and made changes, then there is no need to feel badly. Move on in your new incarnation. Be thankful to your river or the divine for these lessons and move on.

Can you let that version of yourself go? You are not that person anymore and have learned from your experiences.

To forgive your mistakes is not to condone your mistakes. **To forgive is simply to see how the old you in your old reality would make such a mistake.** Perhaps you were naive. Perhaps you were hungry for attention, or scared of the world, or vulnerable because of trauma or your life stage. Perhaps you were afraid of something, or seeking validation. You were certainly human. Call it out for the mistake it was. Recognize why you did it. Feel the regret, make changes to ensure better decisions and close that chapter.

Your suffering in repeated regret, visiting the past over and over, wishing it was different... is a waste of your time and energy. You cannot change the past. But you can design your future.

> *Call it out for the mistake it was. Recognize why you did it. Feel the regret, make changes to ensure better decisions and close that chapter.*

Lastly, accept yourself as human. You were human in the past and you made mistakes. **You are human now. And you will be human in the future.** You are, and will always be, capable of making mistakes. Understanding and accepting your humanity will actually make you a better decision maker. Knowing you are vulnerable to mistakes, you will make decisions carefully, with as much information as you can get. You will learn to trust your gut. And you will learn to analyze your motivations.

> *Knowing you are vulnerable to mistakes, you will make decisions carefully, with as much information as you can get. You will learn to trust your gut. And you will learn to analyze your motivations.*

You are not perfect. You are perfectly human. You can learn to make better choices, learn to let go of the past, and design your future. **Over time your decisions will get better and your mistakes fewer and farther between.** And you will remain perfectly human. Can you leave the past behind and be present for the human you are today?

Connecting To Your Heart - Breaking The Trance Of Unworthiness

We all begin with a sense of unworthiness, somewhere around Stage Two. When you are an infant, your parents love you no matter how much you cry, or make a mess. But, as Tony Robbins points out, that stops around two years old. You can no longer cry all you want, make all the messes you want, and generally be annoying. From this point on, you parents' love and positive attention has conditions on your behavior and your choices. This separation is painful. It seeds us with the idea that maybe we are not worthy of the truly unconditional love that we crave. This is called the trance of unworthiness. But it is a trance that you must break. That does not mean being egotistical or thinking you are higher than everyone else. It means seeing that we are all worthy, yourself included. Not only are we worthy, we all already carry the divine light of love and the divine itself inside of us. This divine light of love and compassion is an infinite source of the unconditional love you crave. And it is a part of you. It always has been. And it always will be.

We are all worthy, yourself included.

So why do we not always feel it? We cover it up. We ignore it. We keep ourselves so busy trying to be what our parents want, what our friends want, or what society wants, all to get that love and attention we crave.

Think about it...

- What do you think others want you to be?
- What do others actually want you to be?
- What do you pretend to be?
- What are you really like?
- Can you look honestly at your strengths and weaknesses?
- Can you see that everyone has strengths and weaknesses?

Affirm this to yourself: **You are not who they want you to be, you are not who you were in the past, you are not who you may pretend to be... you just are; a human in this existence, on this path, just like everyone else.** And that is OK.

If the idea that you are worthy of love is hard to see, you may need to practice feeling love and compassion for yourself each day. You can include this as part of your mediation or prayer, or as a separate exercise. With practice, it will happen more automatically. But do not ever doubt that you are worthy of love just as you are, and you have the power to fill that need for yourself.

Try to feel the divine light physically inside your heart. See that you are worthy of your own love and of the infinite love inside you. You don't have to be anything more or different than what you already are.

Imagine someone who you think is so very worthy of love. They may walk around feeling so unworthy of that love. That probably seems absurd to you. They are so wonderful. Sure, they have their flaws and imperfections. But they are so worthy of your love! If only they could see themselves the way you see them. Imagine that person is you. It is no different. Step back from your human self for a moment and see that you are so wonderful! Sure, you have your flaws and imperfections, but you are so worthy of the love inside you!

Do not ever doubt that you are worthy of love just as you are, and you have the power to fill that need for yourself.

Become the parent figure for yourself that loves you unconditionally. As you take care of yourself and others, love yourself as you love others. Feel that love coming from the divine light inside your heart. Divine love for others.... divine love for you as part of humanity... all together as one humanity worthy of love... and there you are as a part of it all, worthy of that divine love just like everyone else.

Connecting To Others - Seeing Yourself In Others

Connecting to others can be challenging. Others are not always kind. When you think of others, whether they are kind or not, it helps to see them as an aspect of yourself. This is not about projecting yourself into them or faking a new persona for them. This is about seeing their reality and how they reflect some part of you from the past or present or even the future.

Try the following....

Consider family, friends, coworkers, and even strangers that you meet in passing. Start with people you like, work your way out to acquaintances, public figures and even people that you do not like at all, including lastly anyone who ever wronged you.

- **What are the defining characteristics of their personalities?**
- **What aspect of you is that a reflection of?**
- **See everyone as a reflection of some aspect of your current, past or future self.**

For example, maybe they are nerdy and you are nerdy too. Maybe they are bad with money and you were once bad with money in the past. Maybe they are selfish and you remember a time when you were selfish too. Maybe they are placed into your reality to remind you of your past flaws and keep you from repeating them. Maybe they are here to hold a mirror up to you to see the best aspects of yourself.

Can you see them as a caricature of some part of your self; past, present or future? Can you imagine that they are here in your reality to show you some aspect of yourself? Can you imagine that you might be a reflection of some part of who they are or might be?

This is a powerful exercise that may leave you feeling surprised at how you now see others. As you go about your day, try to see this in everyone you meet... ask yourself, what aspect are they showing me? Something from my past? Present? Future? Be grateful to the divine for this gift that shows you about yourself everywhere you go.

Can you see them as a caricature of some part of your self; past, present or future? Can you imagine that you might be a reflection of some part of who they are or might be?

You will find that, as you look into the eyes of others, seeking what is the same between you, you will naturally form deeper connections, forgive more easily, and have more compassion for yourself and others.

While you are holding them in your mind, seeking this sameness, connect to the divine light inside them. Even if they deny their light to the world through cruel actions, the light is there all the same. Maybe evident, maybe buried deep, maybe it busts out of them daily and maybe they push it down. But it's there...

Seeking what is the same between you, you will naturally form deeper connections.

As you seek how they reflect you, **consciously choose to connect** to the divine light inside each person you meet. You will be amazed at the results.

Connecting To Others - Forgiving And Accepting Others As Human

Holding on to a grudge only hurts YOU. Forgiving and accepting others as human - even the people you don't like - is they key to moving on from your past and avoiding new grudges in the future. This does not mean that you condone their actions. This means that you do not choose to make their choices your business. You choose to see them as human and therefore they make mistakes just like you. It also means recognizing that, although they may reflect certain aspects of you, the actions of others have nothing else to do with you. They do not imply anything about you. **A person's actions only implicate themselves.** Let them go.

This does not mean that you condone their actions. This means that you do not choose to make their choices your business. They do not imply anything about you.

Try this... imagine someone who has wronged you. Do you want to give up your time and attention to this person? Or would you be better served by letting the past go? Yes, it was wrong what they did. Yes, it hurt you. Depending on the severity of the wrong, maybe they deserve to be punished. Never fear. Karma will have its way, and you do not have to help it. Allow yourself the grace of letting go.

Can you see how, given their past, their stage at the time, their circumstances, and their flaws, they might act that way? You are probably smarter now and would not let it happen again. Be thankful for this hard lesson. Recognize that this lesson changed you and helped you grow. Now let it go. Do not choose to waste your time on this anymore. You have so much more important work to do.

Recognize that this lesson changed you and helped you grow. Now let it go. You have so much more important work to do.

But what if there is a group of people who wishes you harm? Or an individual who threatens you? You should not be naive. People in Stage Three and Stage Five who may also have specific psychological issues, can be very dangerous. Take steps to protect yourself. But once you have adequate protection in place, let them go from your daily life. This too is human. **There will always be those who wish others harm just as there are those who wish others peace and joy.** No, there is nothing you can do to change their intent. Protect yourself and live your life in peace and joy. Focus on your purpose and tasks at hand.

Forgiving and accepting other individuals as human, or as a natural part of humanity, and letting their actions be their own business, is an important first step that frees your time and attention for better things. The next challenge is to forgive and accept the existence of aspects of society that you previously rejected (groups of people, norms/standards, societal rules, etc).

That does not necessarily mean agreeing with them. It means accepting that they exist and letting it go. It means recognizing that the existence of people, norms, and rules that you may choose to disagree with has no bearing on you - their existence does not imply anything about you. Their existence, and your subsequent disagreement with them does not mean you are wrong or they are right. The fact that groups of people, norms and societal rules exist that you choose to differ from is part of a natural balance in life. Like the concept of Yin and Yang, it takes all kinds to make a complete humanity. **You can disagree, and choose to run your life differently, without demonizing others, or their rules and norms.** They do not have to be wrong, for you to be right. Just let them be different.

If you find yourself feeling offended or lashing out at other people, groups of people, norms or societal rules, remind yourself that all anger is rooted in fear. Ask yourself... **what are you afraid of?** Be brutally honest. Shining a light on your fear will help it leave.

Who do you need to forgive or accept as part of humanity?

They do not have to be wrong, for you to be right. Just let them be different.

Stage Seven: Questioning Everything

*Reality cracked
My foundation broken
Wide open
I am wrong
You are wrong
Society, sobriety
And your rules
Are wrong
Everything popular
Everything brought before
Wrong
And nothing to be done
Come rapture
Come ruin
And the only thing true is
The falsehood
Of everything between
The cracks*

Characteristics

- In an effort to understand what you are missing, you question everything.
- You realize that happiness cannot be found in the outside world. This is a source of disappointment but also of hope.
- You reject ALL ideologies for now, while you question them.
- Previous doubts become meaningful, actionable questions.
- Sometimes you feel lonely because others are still devoted to their ideologies and they don't understand why you are questioning it.
- You tend to question and undertake this stage in private because of the risk of being alienated from your friends and/or communities.

Challenges

DO NOT MAKE ANY DRASTIC CHANGES IN THIS STAGE! Your best course is to try and not do anything stupid during this phase - no major purchases, no new debt, no job changes, no relationship changes, ... until you make it to Stage Eight and have stability and a clearer mind. Stage Seven is all about tearing down everything that everyone else told you life should be and what you should do, questioning that, and deciding for yourself what you want your self and your life to be. You will want to define that clearly before you make any major changes other than nutrition, exercise, and meditation or prayer. Get through this stage as fast as you can but COMPLETE it so that you will not be pulled back here very often.

This is by far the hardest stage. If you have baggage from your childhood, or past experiences that you have not addressed before, this is where you will have to deal with it. If you can be a bit of a hermit during this stage you may thank yourself later.

This stage is also where you are most likely to be depressed and to feel hopeless or that life is pointless. Existential crises are normal here. Understand that this is a natural part of your development and it will pass with time and effort.

Because of the existential nature of this stage, it is more important than ever to maintain connection to your mind, body, self, others, needs, etc. Keep up your efforts to save money, improve your nutrition, maintain some kind of exercise or movement, and all the other skills you have gathered so far.

Tasks

☐ **Connect to your faith** - Understand that questioning your religion is deep exploration that can bring your closer to the divine.

☐ **Question everything**... Religious teachings, social standards, political stances, societal norms, life choices, your lifestyle, your work…(Do not try to make others join you in this questioning if they are not ready. This is YOUR journey, not theirs.)

Connect to yourself...

☐ Practice being mindful of your thoughts and feelings.

☐ Identify the beliefs about yourself, your life, others and your world put into your mind by your parents, friends, and society. Decide if they are right for you.

☐ Identify your own behaviors that are sabotaging you (refresh your efforts to find and break negative patterns from Stage Four)

☐ Dig deep to uncover your own pain from the past and work through it.

☐ Decide who and what you want to be - more caring? Complete unto yourself? At peace? Quiet your mind and ask how you can achieve these in a healthy way.

☐ **Connect to the infinite silence / divine.**

Don't forget to:

☐ Stay connected to your body, movement, sexuality, health, energy and feelings.

☐ Stay connected to your money - resist debt in any form, maintain your savings engine and save for your dreams.

☐ Maintain your needs.

☐ Update your principles and ideology as new experiences shape you.

☐ See and accept your own humanity and the humanity of others.

Resources

- *Don't Sweat The Small Stuff* by Richard Carlson, Ph.D.
- *How To Stop Worrying and Start Living* by Dale Carnegie
- *Play It Away* by Charlie Hoehen
- *Sway* by Ori Brafman and Rom Brafman
- *The Subtle Are Of Not Giving A F*ck* by Mark Manson
- The Tony Robbins Podcast
- *The Tim Ferriss Show* Podcast
- *Letters From A Stoic* by Seneca
- *The Obstacle Is The Way* by Ryan Holiday

Questions To Fuel Your Thinking

- How can you be more kind to yourself?

- What unfinished business do you have? Baggage, limiting beliefs, forgiveness?

- Who do you want to be?

- What do you want your life to FEEL like?

- Can you sense deep in yourself, the infinite peace that the universe/divine put inside you? Can you connect to that?

- What survived your questioning? What are the right beliefs, principles, standards, work and lifestyles for YOU right now?

Connecting To Your Faith Through Questioning

In this stage, you question everything. That includes your religion or faith. This stage is often called **the dark night of the soul**. It is important to understand that questioning your faith is something that every human experiences at some point in their lives. It is a natural part of the cycle of human development. If you believe in a deity that made humanity, then this questioning must have been their intent. Why would any deity want to be questioned? To bring you closer.

Just as a child must grow up and establish a new, deeper relationship with their parents, so too must you now evolve and establish a new and deeper relationship with your faith.

This natural phase of your human existence is an opportunity to get to know your faith in a new and deeper way. Understand that questioning your religion is not going against it - questioning your religion is deep exploration that can bring you closer to your beliefs, or refine them in ways that will bring you closer to the divine. Just as a child must grow up and establish a new, deeper relationship with their parents, so too must you now evolve and establish a new and deeper relationship with your faith.

This new relationship will take some time to fully develop. **The first step towards that new connection has already happened. You are starting to question.** You see the cracks and you are not completely comfortable with them. You can remain in this uncomfortable state with your faith indefinitely, or you can actively walk towards better understanding and deeper connection.

Allow yourself to question all aspects of your faith, but keep it to yourself. This is your own private exploration. Question customs, beliefs, rituals, teachings, historical accounts, etc. Read the history for yourself. Read all the scriptures for yourself. Allow for their historical context and make your own interpretations. Allow your own understanding to evolve with these direct experiences. And for now, just keep exploring, researching and respectfully questioning.

With each aspect that you choose to explore, ask yourself.... **how did it come to be that way? Would you interpret that the same way? Should it still be that way? And most importantly, what is right for you?**

Read the history for yourself. Read all the scriptures for yourself. Allow for their historical context and make your own interpretations. Allow your own understanding to evolve with these direct experiences. And for now, just keep exploring, researching and respectfully questioning.

Connecting To Doubt - Questioning Everything

As you question everything, remember to include **religious teachings, social standards, political stances, societal norms, life choices, your lifestyle, your work, future plans, nutrition, exercise, sexuality and literally everything else**... let nothing be immune from your exploration.

Let nothing be immune from your exploration. Question if it is true, or right for you, or what you really want, or what parts align with you or not.

Question if it is true, or right for you, or what you really want, or what parts align with you or not. To fuel your thinking, read and explore what others have found the answers to be, but focus on what the answer is for YOU.

As you explore and question things more directly, and form your own interpretations, you will have some challenges...

You and your spouse, family or friends may end up in very different places. You may come to conclusions that are different from the people around you. As a result, your family and friends may change dramatically. But if you can, let it be. This is an opportunity to practice being connected to others who have different ideas. Can you let their beliefs be theirs and let yours be yours? If you are so different, that it causes conflict or if they are in Stage Five and feel the need to attack you for feeling differently, you may need some time away. If you discover that certain relationships are abusive or certain people in your life are dangerous, remove yourself quickly. For more subtle toxicity, fade away slowly and quietly. Time changes us all and one day you may want to reconnect, when you have both evolved. **Avoid drama in either case.**

Time changes us all and one day you may want to reconnect, when you have both evolved.

Equally challenging, you may find that areas of your life need reshaping based on your evolving beliefs. Because this stage involves rapid and continual evolution, try to keep changes to a minimum until you are through it. If you make changes too early, you may evolve yet again and find yourself in a chaotic race to keep up with your own changing beliefs. **In general, if safety is not a concern, wait until Stage Eight to make any drastic changes in relationships and careers.**

Next, do not try to make others join you in this questioning if they are not ready. This is YOUR journey, not theirs. They might see your questioning as a threat. They might fear losing you from their lives as you evolve. They may feel lesser because they are not questioning. None of these possibilities leads to anything good. So keep your thoughts to yourself for now.

This is YOUR journey, not theirs.

Remember that in this stage, you will cycle though many ideological changes. Try not to settle on any one belief set too adamantly before you have explored all of its cracks and inconsistencies. For a while, you will be jumping between new beliefs like stepping stones. Do not cling to any one of them too tightly. Just think, "This will do for now."

So how will you know when you have landed on the right, magical combination of religious, social, moral, political and other beliefs that fit you ideally and you can finally move on to Stage Eight? **You will have completed Stage Seven's questioning when your ideology is a simple set of overarching principles (rather than specific rules and issues)**, and these principles are the same as those at the heart of all religions, all societies, and all humanity.

Now get out there and explore everything. Ask yourself what is common to all religions? What is common to all societies? What is common to all humanity? What principles can you find there that work for you?

Connecting To Yourself - Healing Your Scars

No one makes it to adulthood without scars. Our bodies and minds are scared from our experiences. **This is not an excuse to be a victim. This is a fact of human existence.** And the scars do not stop coming just because we reach eighteen. Life keeps happening. And it drapes onto us emotional baggage; scars that ache when triggered by what feels like the past. How did they get there? It is a simple amygdala response. If ever anything scared you, threatened you, or simply landed you in a bad situation, your amygdala responds by creating a permanent record; a scar in your mind. Every time you encounter a similar situation, that scar will activate, warning you to avoid repeating the same mistakes. It sounds like a great system.

It makes us assume the worst, expect the worst from others, and it blinds us to the beauty of our current reality.

The problem with this built-in survival mechanism is that it makes us act irrationally. It makes us treat our new spouse like they are the old partner every time the new spouse does something that reminds us of some distant past situation. It makes us feel unsafe when we really are safe now. Worst of all, it makes us preemptively lash out at just the hint of the possibility of past similarity. It makes us assume the worst, expect the worst from others, and it blinds us to the beauty of our current reality. It keeps us living in the past, and worrying about the future.

However, you can heal these emotional scars. The process is simple, but not always easy.

First, **practice being mindful of your thoughts and feelings**. When you feel any strong negative emotion, recognize it. Name it. You might find that your baggage has a signature way of appearing. For example, do you notice a trend that if you are yelling, or crying, that baggage is at the root?

Then, **detach from it and explore it** for what it can teach you. Ask yourself ...

- What am I feeling?
- Why?... why?..... why? .... keep asking until you find the real cause.
- What am I afraid of? (Fear is at the heart of all negative emotions. Ultimately, you are afraid of some situation that happened in the past and you are afraid it will happen again and afraid of seeing the same consequences.)
- What baggage is this from my past?
- Is this relevant? Is this really likely to happen here and now? If the answer is no, then breathe deep and release it.

Thank this fear for protecting you but you don't need it anymore.

If you do not like the idea of waiting for your emotional baggage to pop up, and you would like to accelerate this process, you can actively dig deep to uncover your own pain from the past and work through it. In other words, **trigger your own baggage, so you can release it.**

There are many ways to do this... you might find a good counselor or therapist. You might find a friend who wants to do the same and help each other. Or you might work alone with a journal.

The trick is to find where the scars might be, and focus on that incident to reveal any leftover issues you have not yet let go of. Think back on your past from day one. What major incidences do you remember? What was your childhood like? Tell your counselor, friend or journal about your friends, what made you angry, what were your parents like, what made you sad? If you were crying back then, what was the most likely reason? What was school like? What traumatic events did you endure?

It is important to remember that traumatic is a relative term. If the child in you thought it was traumatic, then it likely created a scar in your mind. Don't ignore it.

Emotional scars and baggage typically form from our relationships with friends, parents, and significant others in childhood and beyond. Related to this are limiting beliefs and self sabotaging behaviors which are addressed in another set of tasks. For now, focus on trauma and other very negative experiences and how they might have created fears in you about specific situations. Include everything right up to your current age.

Unpacking your emotional baggage is like peeling an onion. As soon as you think you have resolved the last bit, something new reveals yet another scar that needs to be healed. Obviously, the more trauma you have endured the more work you have ahead of you. This will be an ongoing effort that lasts beyond this stage, but it is easier and occurs less often with time.

Recognize it.

Name it.

Explore it.

Release it.

Connecting To Yourself - Identifying And Replacing Limiting Beliefs

While you are questioning your ideology and beliefs about the world, it is a great time to **identify and question the beliefs about yourself and your life, put into your mind by your parents, friends, and society**, and to decide if they are right for you. We are looking for limiting beliefs. These are beliefs that hold you back from doing what you feel compelled to do. Limiting beliefs are inherently negative. They are beliefs about what you are not, what you cannot be, or what you are not capable of. Limiting beliefs might sound like the voice of your parents, siblings, or childhood friends, labeling you as something negative.

Limiting beliefs can also come from just watching your parents as a child. How did your parents act towards each other? What beliefs might this have implanted in you?

Try this...

1. List any beliefs that come to mind.

2. Then, decide what you will replace them with. For each limiting belief, make a supportive belief that will support your efforts instead.

3. Then, read your new beliefs every day for at least a month or more to retrain your brain.

4. You might consider using a spaced repetition flash card system app, or posting your list where you can see it every day.

Limiting beliefs are inherently negative. They are beliefs about what you are not, what you cannot be, or what you are not capable of.

Limiting beliefs put in us as children can be VERY hard to get rid of. If **you find that you have some limiting beliefs that you just cannot fully replace, try adding on to them, to make them positive** instead of negative. For example, here is a list of common limiting beliefs and an additional phrase for each that makes it positive...

- I am strange or weird.... unique and amazing.
- I do not belong... among people who hold me back.
- No one will listen... if they are not ready. Don't force them.
- I am self-centered... centered securely in my own soul.
- The way I want to do it will not work... unless I actually do it. So do it.
- Nobody listens to women... who do not speak up. So speak up.

- I am a silly child... playful and inquisitive like the purity of childhood.
- What I want is irrelevant... until I decide otherwise.

So if you have some limiting beliefs holding you back and you cannot seem to get rid of them, try completing them instead. Remember to read it often to retrain your brain.

If you find that you have some limiting beliefs that you just cannot fully replace, try adding on to them instead, to make them positive instead of negative.

Connecting To The Infinite Silence / Divine

There is, within you, an infinite silence. You might call it the divine, or God, or Allah, or The Tao or anything else. It is the divine presence within you. Every religion and philosophy (except maybe humanism) includes a concept that the divine is in our hearts, or that we should welcome the divine into ourselves. When the same idea shows up in every religion, it is often correct. **Within your finite physical being is what can only be described as an infinite space of sentient silence or divine light.**

Sitting in meditation or prayer, scan your body from the top down. Just explore what it feels like inside. Maybe there are some tight muscles, or pain here and there, or maybe you can feel your recent meal digesting or your heart beating. Focus consciously on what is happening inside your body. Take your attention from the top of your head slowly down all the way to your toes. This kind of somatic mindfulness is a great meditation by itself. But today, let's take it further. Today, when you reach your belly, notice if you find one particular spot where, when you place your attention on it with curious openness, opens into a seemingly infinite space of silence and compassion and acceptance. This spot is sometimes referred to as the lower dantian (or dantien). There is a lot of interesting writing to explore about the upper, middle and lower dantians. Connecting with the lower dantian can have some fascinating effects.

Find one particular spot where, when you place your attention on it with curious openness, it opens into a seemingly infinite space of silence and compassion and acceptance.

If you can connect with and open this infinite space within you, you can **imagine sinking into it like you are sinking into a hot tub.** But here is the thing… To really connect with the infinite silence, you must come with nothing. After all, it is hard to connect with the nothing, if you show up laden with somethings. Imagine, as you scan down your body, that all the worries of the day are like backpacks and bags draped around you. Take them off and put them down. All the worries, all the roles we play, all the responsibilities and fears and expectations. Put them all down. Put down this person living this life. Take off this human existence. Approach the infinite silence as nothing more than your inner true self - the silent observer.

Meet this infinite divine space with only your divine soul. It is such a place of peace. There are no expectations here; no attachments, no roles, no responsibilities, no identity, no physical being. Nothing but pure consciousness in the moment. **This is the perfect space to drop in a wish for anything you might want to bring into your life.** Think of what you would like to happen in your life.

Take the need for it, the desire or want for it, and give over that desire to the infinite divine knowing that, if it is in line with your purpose, of course it will be.

> *There are no expectations here; no attachments, no roles, no responsibilities, no identity, no physical being.*

Many religions encourage their followers to, "Let go and let God." - that is, to give over what they want to the divine and let the divine bring it to you, knowing that if you ask, you shall receive. Connecting to the infinite silence / divine is about understanding that the divine is quite literally within you and you can access it, make requests, and feel its infinite acceptance anytime you like. It is not out there in some nebulous place. The divine is right here, inside you, right now.

For the more scientific mind, it helps to think back to the big bang. **At first, there was nothing, and out of that infinite silence came the universe.** The universe is full of dichotomies. So it is only natural that all the something that we see around us came out of the nothing. **And that within the something that is ourselves, is the nothing that created it all.** Us in the universe and the universe within us. Sit quietly, contemplate that and see where it takes you.

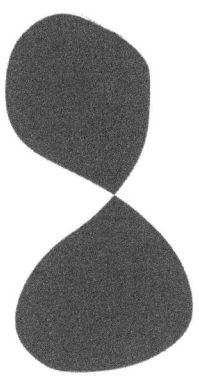

Stage Eight: I Am A Child Of The Universe/Divine

Dig deeper
Through the cracks
Came the light
See here
The pieces
Broken down
The mosaic
Laid now
Before me
See the truth
The connected roots
Dig deeper
Because the truth
Is never on the surface
Return to this
To the ancient
Truth
Whispering
In every breath
We inhale

Characteristics

- You cycle through several belief sets trying to find one that fits and then eventually, instead of rejecting all ideologies, you actively examine them to find what parts are true.
- You see connections and relationships between ideologies.
- You see the interdependent truth at the heart of all ideologies and use THAT to anchor yourself.
- You surrender to not knowing all the answers.

Challenges

In this stage it it now much safer to begin designing your ideal life and making changes. Think through those changes carefully. Take your time so that you might be able to implement your ideal life more efficiently and effectively.

TASKS

- [ ] **Connect to the universal truth.**

- [ ] **Connect to the Silent Observer.**

- [ ] **Connect to your reality** - design your future.

- [ ] **Connect to your purpose** - identify it.

- [ ] **Connect to others** - can you see their truth now? Can you see their heart? Can you see their humanity? Can you see what stage they are in at the moment? Practice!

Don't forget to:

- [ ] Stay connected to your body - movement, feelings, energy, sexuality, health.

- [ ] Stay connected to your money - resist debt in any form, maintain your savings engine and save for your dreams.

- [ ] Maintain your needs.

- [ ] Update your principles and ideology as new experiences shape you.

- [ ] See and accept your own humanity and the humanity of others.

- [ ] Question everything and seek the honest truth, even if it does not agree with your current ideologies or what you would hope is the truth.

- [ ] Connect to the infinite peace/divine inside you.

Questions To Fuel Your Thinking

- With any decision you make, what is the emotional root of this choice? Fear? Greed? Joy? Purpose? Be honest with yourself. Avoid decisions based on negative emotions.

- What do you want your life to be? What do you want to FEEL?

- What is your purpose here? What is your unique contribution to this world?

Resources

- *The War of Art* By Steven Pressfield
- *The 4 Hour Work Week* by Tim Ferriss
- *Wherever You Go There You Are* by Jon Kabatt Zinn
- *The Crossroads of Should and Must* by Elle Luna
- *The Art of Everyday Ecstasy* by Margot Anand
- *Dangerous Personalities* by Joe Navarro
- *The Laws Of Human Nature* by Robert Greene

Connecting To Universal Truths

As you read, think and grow, take note of what is common among all beliefs, among all religions, among all political ideologies, etc. - What are the connections or relationships between them?

At first, common themes will be hard to find. For example, political ideologies from the left and the right or religions from different parts of the world might seem so completely different that they have nothing in common at all. The key to seeing the common basis for them all is to stop looking at the level of specific rules, specific beliefs and specific issues and focus instead on principles, and even one level higher than that... focus on the emotional roots of the principles.

> *As you read, think and grow, take note of what is common among all beliefs, among all religions, among all political ideologies, etc. - What are the connections or relationships between them?*

For example, Christianity and Islam might seem very far apart. But can we find something common to them both? They both have one deity, and this deity is personified, and they each say we are children of the deity, and in certain portions of post-crusades writings, they both advocate brotherly love for all humanity. Now let's add in something like Taoism.

What is common to all three? Taoism does not have a personified deity, so we will have to move upwards in our perspective and say that they all three suggest there is a single all powerful force which creates everything and we are descended of that one force and that one force is the embodiment of love. They also all say that this one divine force is in our hearts or within us. This is just one interpretation.

Form your own exploration of what abstract truths are at the heart of all religions. Then consider what abstract truths are at the heart of all political ideologies. Then consider what abstract truths are common to all humanity. What do most people want out of life? What do most people worry about?

When you connect with the abstract truths common to all ideologies and all humanity, this does not mean you are giving up your current political ideology, or your current religion. It just means you are recognizing that there is something true at the heart of them all. Each religion and each political ideology and all humans then apply these truths in wildly different ways to make decisions about everyday life and who to vote for. How you choose to apply them might be very different from how someone else chooses.

The more we see that we are not so different, the easier it is to live and let live. It becomes easier to agree to disagree about the particular applications and implications of those truths. If you are not very religious, start there and work your way to the harder topics where you feel most deeply entrenched.

There is something true at the heart of them all. Each religion and each political ideology and all humans then apply these truths in wildly different ways to make decisions.

As you find the truths behind all ideologies, and the common desires of all people, write them down and think about them. Let them deepen your connection to others, the divine, your faith, and your principles.

Connecting To The Universe / Divine - Letting Go Of Knowing

Some of us are comfortable with not knowing anything and never asking the big questions. That must be somewhat liberating; but perhaps unsatisfying.

For some of us, simple, findable and somewhat mundane information is comforting. We want to know the future so that we can make better decisions or know how something is going to turn out. Do you like to know what to expect each week? Who is planning what, the details on each and every event, and how it will all play out? That is a lot of expectation.

Expectation is a dangerous form of attachment. Planning for the future is good, but feeling too certain about it is not. You should plan, but you must let go of expecting things to actually go that way. We cannot know the future. Knowing what is happening right now is hard enough. Let go of knowing the future.

Now that you can trust the river of your life, the next step is to trust that the answers you need will come when you need them.

But **to be human is to want to know**. Once we let go of wanting to know the future, we often evolve to wanting to know the truth. We want to know the truth behind all sorts of things. We want to know how life works and what is on the other side. Some of these questions have answers that are easily found. Some of these questions have answers that take some work (like the answers you will find by working through this roadmap). And some questions do not have answers right now.

Now that you can trust the river of your life, the next step is to trust that the answers you need will come when you need them.

If you are academically minded, this can be very hard to accept. The quest for answers is as human as the quest for love and acceptance. This does not mean that we should not seek answers. It means that while you work toward the answers, **be comfortable in not knowing yet, or not knowing right now.** Be comfortable in the fact that you do not know everything and for right now, you do not need to know. In fact, you don't know much at all in the grand scheme of the universe and never will. And that is OK.

You will seek the answers to many questions. You will find some answers easily, others answers with work, and some you will never know. And that is not just OK, that is human.

Trusting that the answers you need will come when you need them is the key to letting go of needing to know right now. Let it be. Plan for your own future.

Work towards answers to the big questions. Let go of needing to know right now... and strangely, the answers will come, right on time.

A common question at this point is wondering HOW the answers will come? The short answer is that they will come to you as you go about your daily life. Sometimes you will be compelled to seek out an answer online, or seek out a new book to read. You might have a conversation with a friend who will suggest a new book or website or local activity or someone they think you would get along with. Your river will either bring you the answer and put it right in front of your face or it will deliver you the resource that has the answer, if only you will be quick enough to act on it. When you are flowing with your river, you will seem to encounter coincidences that bring you answers as you follow the trail like a detective.

Work towards answers to the big questions. Let go of needing to know right now... and strangely, the answers will come, right on time.

Be open to reading that book, doing that search, attending that local activity or talking to that recommended person. Listen within those results for the whisper of your river taking you where you need to be and bringing you the answers you need. When the answers come, thank your river/universe/divine for bringing that into your life. Feel gratitude for receiving the answer, and more answers will come.

Connecting To The Silent Observer

When you wake up, it's like someone else is looking through your eyes at you. This is the silent observer. If you have not yet met the silent observer, allow me to introduce you. **First, read this to yourself, quietly in your head … "Hello there."** Now, who said that? You might say that you said it to yourself. But your lips did not move and your vocal chords did not make a sound. But you said it. And you heard it. You said it without a voice and you heard it without needing ears. And if you wanted to, you could imagine and relive your past or imagine your future and see it without using your eyes. You just did that.

There is the you that is this body and quite separately, there is the you that speaks and listens and sees without needing this body at all.

There is the you that is this body and quite separately, there is the you that speaks and listens and sees without needing this body at all. This you is a combination of the mind and the silent observer. The mind thinks and expresses and imagines and feels. The silent observer observes and directs from deep inside. Can you feel the difference? If you quiet the mind, can you feel something present inside you? Something quiet but very present that observes and experiences this life like a video game player within an avatar? You might call it your soul. It is tempting to call it your true being, but **here you are on this earth in this life, in this body with this mind and these energies and this silent observer and all of it together is what it is to be a human being.**

You are a physical being, a mind being, an energy being and a silent being, all at the same time. The best results come when we acknowledge and find connection to each of these.

The mind thinks and expresses and imagines and feels. The silent observer observes and directs from deep inside.

The silent observer is arguably the hardest to connect to because it is … silent. The cacophony of everyday life is so loud that we often don't connect with this inner being. To connect with the silent observer, first simply quiet your mind enough to feel the silent observer within you. Feel how you are not your body, but you are in your body and you observe your body and you operate your body. Next, Feel how you have a mind. Watch the thoughts and feelings go by like clouds in the sky, but see that you are not your mind; you observe your mind and you operate your mind. So who are you? You are what is left. The essence of you is the silent observer that is here in this life, operating this body, this mind and these energies. Perhaps the silent observer is made of energy too (because it does not seem to be made of physical matter).

Connecting to that self in this way opens up a perspective that you can use to take control of your mind, body and energies and use them like an avatar, to create whatever life you want. **Practice being the Silent Observer in your daily life and note the difference in how you react, experience, and think.**

Connecting To Your Purpose - Methods For Finding It

Finding your purpose or mission in life is not easy, precisely because it it unique to you. You cannot look at other people, like a menu of options, and expect to find your purpose there. When you look at others and their purpose, you may be looking at a list of what your purpose is NOT. You may need to invent a task, vocation or mission that is completely new to this world - you have never seen anything exactly like it and neither has anyone else. That's hard because we are not necessarily taught to do that. However, you are certainly capable.

There are a lot of good methods out there for finding your unique purpose. Try them all until you find one that works for you and/or you spot a pattern or connection in the results… here they are:

Free Flow Writing - Get a bank piece of paper or pull up a blank note on your device (whichever will allow you to get ideas down the fastest). Start by asking yourself, "What is my purpose?," or, "What is my mission in life?" Then, write whatever comes to mind. Just start listing ideas and keep listing until you get to something that makes you cry. An emotional response is the key to spotting the right answer.

Intersections - Write down four separate lists: (1) What you are good at (2) What you enjoy (3) What the world needs and (4) what you can get paid for. Your purpose or mission in life is at the intersection of these four things. Now, your purpose in life may not necessarily be linked to an income. If, however, you are doing this exercise because you want a new career, and you are not yet financially free, then include what you can get paid for.

Try them all until you find one that works for you and/or you spot a pattern or connection in the results.

What Have You Always Done? - In this exercise, you look back from childhood until now and ask yourself what have you always done, when nobody is looking, when you are not getting paid for it, etc. What MUST you do just because you cannot imagine not doing it? What activities are at the core of your being and always have been since your youngest days?

Skills Assessment - Ask people you trust (and who would tell you honestly) to list the skills that you are really really really good at. Which of your best skills gives you joy? How can you invest in and possibly combine those skills?

The Simon Sinek Method - Call a small number of your closest friends (people that have known you a long time). Ask each of them, "Why are you my friend?". They may have a hard time and need to think about that, to really get to the heart of it. But keep digging and they will eventually have an epiphany about how you make them FEEL or some other thing that you do for their INTERNAL self. This is the value that you bring to humanity. How can you leverage that into a purpose, mission or vocation?

The Tony Robbins Method - Tony Robbins has lots of very insightful methods for everything and this is no exception. When you were very young (3-5 years old), what did you want to be when you grew up? WHY? When you were a teenager, what did you want to be for a career? WHY? When you were in your twenties, what did you want to be for a career? WHY? Thirties?…. keep going until you reach your present age. Then, focus on all the WHYs. What is the pattern in the why? Can you combine the whys into one purpose, mission or vocation?

Sit Down, Shut Up & Listen - In this method, you simply ask for the answer and it is delivered to you. This is also called mediation, prayer, or as Jesse Elder puts it, Cosmic Google. It is wonderfully effective, although it takes some practice. Find a quiet place where you can be alone and will be guaranteed to be undisturbed for a period of time… let's say 15-60 minutes. Turn off your devices and get your typical distractions as far away from you as possible. Sit down. Quiet your mind by listening to the silence intently. Ask your question; in this case, "What is my mission?," or, "What is my purpose?". Wait patiently for the answer and write it down exactly as you hear it - do not stop to interpret it. And don't dismiss it. Think about how it fits in with what you found from the other methods.

Remember, your result may not look exactly like anything you have seen before, so if it looks exactly like something someone else is doing, you need to be more specific and carry out your mission in a more unique way or by a new method. Get creative!

Connecting To Your Reality - Designing Your Future

The time has come to start designing what you want your life to be like. Why now? At this point, your ideology should be principle-based and therefore stable, your emotional baggage is mostly unpacked, and you are ready to focus on fulfillment and purpose rather than ego and impulse. That is not to say that you should not get that dream car, if you can pay cash for it, but you will find that designs that further your purpose are easily granted, whereas requests that further your ego and insecurities are often denied. As always, be aware of the emotional roots of your choices, because the result will multiply those emotions. Be sure to design from a place of peace, love, joy, adventure or other positive emotions.

> *Be aware of the emotional roots of your choices, because the result will multiply those emotions.*

This should be a fun and joyous exercise and one you will want to revisit often. Consider all aspects: mental, emotional, intellectual, physical, career, relationships, daily schedule, financial, experiences, opportunities, etc. **What does your ideal life look like?** Be very, very specific and brutally honest about your ideal life, even if it sounds unreasonable. **Many things are easier than you think.**

Your ideal life may not look like something your family or friends would approve of. It may not look like the standard definition of success that we are all handed in school. That is OK. Do not design the life that you were told to want. Design the life that makes your soul sing. Design the life that makes your whole being burst forth with energy and makes your heart feel full to overflowing.

> *Design the life that makes your soul sing.*

Write it all down. This is key. Then, for each element of your ideal life, research what it would take to make it happen. Don't take any one person's word on the matter. Study it from all sides on your own, and talk to as many experts as you can find. Then, start making it happen.

Review the process for manifesting from Stage Two and use it here as well.

Connecting To Others - Seeing Their Truth

You have come a long way now and know a lot about the universal truths that drive humanity. You have connected deeply with yourself, the Divine and your reality. You have connected to others in terms of their needs, possibly in terms of sexuality, and certainly in terms of seeing their humanity. Now it is time to see their truth.

When you next see a friend or family member, consciously connect with them. Reach out your energy towards them with the intent to connect. Intend to be open. When you do, ask to be shown their truth. You are putting yourself in their shoes energetically. You will be able to feel their current emotions, and and state of mind.

Can you see their truth now? Can you see their heart or intentions? Can you see their humanity? Can you see what stage they are in at the moment? Practice!

Reach out your energy towards them with the intent to connect. Intend to be open. When you do, ask to be shown their truth.

Try the same technique as you pass strangers on the street. You do not need to stare at them, just a glance and the intent to reach out and connect with your energy is enough.

If they catch your eye, smile and send them peace, joy or whatever you feel they need... all as you pass by.

Just because you can see people's truth and intentions, and just because you send them joy and peace, does not mean that everyone you meet will be kind. There will always be people in earlier stages who cannot see your humanity yet and may do you harm. But if you can see the truth of their intentions, you can protect yourself. **By connecting with others in this way, you can better understand them, better protect yourself, and better help those in need, all at the same time**.

No, you are not reading minds. Humans project their intentions and state of mind openly. We cannot help sending out a signal to everyone around us, detailing our truth. You are just learning to tune in to that, connect to that channel, and send something positive and helpful back.

This is particularly helpful because many people hide their pain and their challenges. Many people suffer in silence. If you can recognize that, you can offer to help, encourage them to talk, or simply send them caring and compassion.

Enjoy this new level of connection and all the good you can do with it!

Stage Nine: I Am A Consciousness Trapped In This Body

Consciousness in breath
Can never be forever
Turn me now
Into the energy
For maybe this
Will save me
From the fear
Of the fear itself
Of the end
And my own
Not knowing
Pure consciousness
Encapsulated
Yes, capitulated
I surrender
This mortal form early
For maybe this
Will save me
From the fear
Of the fear
Of self separated
From self

Characteristics

- You see religions, people, ideologies, places, and everything as one coherent whole with love at the heart of it all.
- You see that there is no self - you are a consciousness separate from your body and can feel the differences between your physical self and your internal consciousness.
- You do not blame anyone for anything happening in your own life.
- You have a sense of your purpose or mission.

Challenges

The major challenge of this stage is to cultivate presence in the NOW. This moment, not the past or the future. It is a good challenge to have, but harder than it sounds. This stage is a beautiful and purpose filled place. The joy of acting on your newfound purpose is overwhelming. At the same time, you can feel guilty about this amazing life you are building. You can feel humbled by this gift of insight and connection. But you cannot end the suffering of others by joining them. You CAN, however, offer peace, joy and the example of a path towards a better life. That being said, do not preach. Just live your joy and shine bright.

TASKS

☐ **Connect to this moment.**

☐ **Connect to your intuition.**

☐ **Connect to your purpose** - make a plan.

☐ **Connect to your intellect** - gather the skills and knowledge you need to forward your purpose.

☐ **Form a more complete connection to your partner.**

Don't forget to:

☐ Stay connected to your body - movement, feelings, energy, sexuality, health.

☐ Stay connected to your money - resist debt in any form, maintain your savings engine and save for your dreams.

☐ Maintain your needs.

☐ Update your principles and ideology as new experiences shape you.

☐ See and accept your own truth and humanity and that of others.

☐ Question everything and seek the honest truth, even if it does not agree with your current ideologies or what you would hope is the truth.

☐ Connect to the infinite peace/divine and silent observer inside you.

Resources

- *The Power of Now* by Eckhart Tolle
- *The First Three Minutes* by Steven Weinberg
- *Intuitive Healing* by Judith Orloff M.D.
- *Fluent Forever* by Gabriel Wyner

Questions To Fuel Your Thinking

- Can you be fully present NOW?

- Can you trust your intuition? What does it tell you?

- How can you manifest your purpose in this world? What skills and knowledge do you need?

- Can you feel the infinite peace and joy inside you? Can you let it flow out of you?

Connecting To This Moment - Presence, Mindfulness and Intuition

Many traditions recommend being present in the now. If worry is about the future and regret is about the past, then being here in the present moment is one way to significantly reduce the worry and regret in your life. That is a great start. But this moment has so much more to show you. Being present in this moment, experiencing it fully, is an opportunity to connect deeply with family, friends, your children or your partner. Your full and complete attention and connection in this moment is the greatest gift you can give.

Further, being present in this moment, you can tap into vast information. Intuition or gut instinct is nothing more than your ability to connect with the infinite information and wisdom in this moment. In this moment, is infinite information about the present state of people, places and things. Anything you could want to know about what is happening right now, you can know: how someone is feeling, their intention, whether you are safe or not, the right thing to do, or what not to do, and more.

To tap into this vast and useful information, **start by being mindful of your surroundings**. That is, pay attention and observe your surroundings in a detached but focused way. What does that mean? You have already connected to the Silent Observer. Watch your surroundings as that Silent Observer. No devices, no distractions... just be here in this moment now, taking in the sights, sounds and feelings around you. Notice people, colors, textures, smells, and every detail. If your mind wanders towards thinking about tomorrow or last week, gently bring it back. This is an active mindfulness. If you are not used to it, it can feel a little intense. Stay with it.

Next, when you feel connected to this moment across all your physical senses, **reach out with an intent to connect with the people here in this moment**. This is just like connecting with other people individually, but this time with a group. Be open. Project your energy out from yourself, to each person around you, painting the group with your energy and presence in a general way as you glance around the space. If this is challenging, try connecting with each individual quickly until you have connected with the group. Our intent in this exercise is not to explore each person's truth, but the truth of the crowd and this space in this moment. You are now connected to everything you can see.

Now here is the challenging part.... **connect with what you cannot see**. Imagine connecting with the energy and presence in the air. Imagine that the air itself is full of the energy of everyone here, of everything here, and of the place itself. Like static energy before a storm, it fills the air. You cannot see it, but you can feel it. This is the energy of the moment; pervasive and touching this moment, all over the world and beyond. Feel how your energy contributes to it, and connects to it.

Now ask your question. What do you want to know? **Questions about the past or future are not going to be answered here.** But anything you could want to know about the state of things right now, or the best choice to make right now, is yours. Remain detached from it - that is, be the Silent Observer, connected to this moment. Let answers come to you. This is your intuition.

1. *Explore the truth of the crowd and this space in this moment.*
2. *Connect to everything you can see.*
3. *Connect to the energy in this moment.*
4. *Ask your question.*
5. *Let the answer come.*

Practice it to make it stronger. When you drive or walk down the street, stay connected to each moment. Read people, places and things in this way, and let your intuition guide you. The more you trust it and use it, the stronger it gets.

Your intuition can guide you on small things, like finding a great restaurant, and in big things like crafting your ideal life. When you are in this moment, fully connected, flowing with your river, your intuition is a constant guide.

Finally, for a more advanced challenge, when deeply connected to this moment, feeling the collective energy of everything and everyone in the space, **can you feel how the people are all the same**; just people, going through life, trying to figure it out, making mistakes, living in stages, all ultimately on the same journey? **Can you see how the things in this space are all the same**... just physical objects all made up of the same basic particles? Can you feel the sameness of the people, the things, and this space ... all made up of the same particles and energies but taking various forms like pixels in a video game? They all look different but are all ultimately just bits of energy. Spend some time thinking about that and feeling it in the moment.

Connecting Completely To Your Partner

Few things are more fulfilling than romantic love. So how can we make it even better? Cultivating a complete connection with your partner, is a gateway to more love, more romance, more play, more fun, more and better sex, and more emotional intimacy. More than that, it is a mechanism to seeing and experiencing the humanity of each other, leading ultimately to both of you evolving further along the Cycle of Human Development, together, accelerating each other's efforts.

To cultivate complete connection, work in order from the ground up to make sure you have a solid foundation and are not missing anything. The chakras make a perfect framework for this mini-cycle of development. **Carry out each task any way you like. Get creative!**

To cultivate complete connection, work in order from the ground up

Root - Connect with your partner through trust, safety and grounding.

☐ Build trust.

☐ Build safety (including bodily autonomy).

☐ Ground each other.

Sacral - Connect with your partner through sexuality, the infinite divine, and the infinite energy. (Note: it helps to be at peace when you come to bed so that you can be a place of peace for each other.)

☐ Connect through sexuality.

☐ Experiment, and be honest.

☐ Feel the infinite silence and energy inside each other, allow it to rise and build.

☐ Give of your energy to each other.

☐ Give of this infinite peace to each other.

Solar Plexus - Connect with your partner's independent will, power, individuality, uniqueness and strength of self. (Note: Be careful of arrogance and power trips centered in your own insecurities.)

☐ Celebrate their uniqueness and quirks.

☐ Encourage their strength of self.

☐ Revel in their journey, how they enjoy their interests.

☐ Take the time to listen without expectation of response.

Heart - Connect with your partner through love and compassion for self and each other.

☐ Try eye gazing, snuggling, hugs, holding hands...

☐ Give compassion for their current challenges - compassion is seeing their humanity as an aspect of yourself, not trying to solve their problems for them, unless they specifically ask for your help or ideas.

☐ Play, flirt, give each other time, attention and priority.

Throat - Connect with your partner's personal truth and expression.

☐ Create an environment between you where speaking your truth is rewarded, praised and encouraged, never judged but held in love and compassion.

☐ Play "Truth Or Truth" - ask each other questions in a private place. No judging. See their answers as an aspect of yourself.

Third Eye - Connect to your partner's higher perception, intuition, and inspiration.

☐ Encourage your partner's development of perception and intuition (if that is their goal).

☐ See your partner's divine nature and purpose.

☐ See them as an angel, god or goddess.

☐ See the light inside that radiates through them.

☐ Create a shared vision of a future that excites you both and has space for you both to grow, explore interests, and fulfill your purposes in shared support.

Crown - Connect to your partner's wisdom, and to your shared oneness and transcendence.

☐ Talk about how you think the world works and how the divine works.

☐ Feel at one with each other.

☐ See how you are the same.

☐ Feel what it is like to be them, feeling what it is like to be you.

☐ Experience shared transcendence by opening to each other and connecting completely along all of these aspects that you have now developed.

Above all, enjoy and have fun creating this deep and complete connection to your partner. Revisit it often to maintain this blissful connection.

Connecting To The One Consciousness

In this stage, you often feel like a consciousness trapped inside this body. You can feel the difference between your body and your consciousness. As you practice connecting to each moment, connecting within that moment to your intuition, and starting to feel the sameness in all things, reach out within that connection, and feel what it it like to be these other people.

Put yourself energetically in their place. **What does it feel like to be them in this moment?** It is a subtle feeling. It is not intense. But if you focus, and practice, you can feel within your gut, what it feels like to be them.

Does it feel confident? Insecure? Joyful? Playful? Sad?

Then, have an open mind here. This exercise has an important point... **feel what it is like to BE** that table, or that chair or that plant. Does it feel stable, heavy, low, tall, fragile, cold, warm, metallic? Can you feel the qualities of the wood or plastic or leaves without touching it?

Spend a little time looking around the room and FEEL what it is like to BE other people, places and things.

If you have completed the previous tasks, you will be surprised to find you can feel it. You can feel what it is like to be anyone, or anything. Previously you could IMAGINE what it was like to be them, or

Spend a little time looking around the room and FEEL what it is like to BE other people, places and things.

at least what you would feel like if that were you, but this is different... you can actually put your energy in their place and FEEL their truth in this moment.

It is time to question... how can you do that? How is it that you can place your consciousness into theirs? How can you step into their consciousness with yours?

Because it is the same consciousness.

Think about the oceans and rivers of the world. They are all connected. Rivers flow into oceans, which flow into other oceans, and connect to other rivers. It is all one big body of water. But, the Mississippi River looks and acts very different from the Caribbean Sea. Why? Local environments significantly influence the nature of these rivers and oceans. Local environments influence how they look, how fast they flow, what fish live there, how they are used and more.

It is the same with people. We are all one big consciousness, but our local environments (as a child and now) influence how we look, how we act, and what we do in this world. We are extensions of the same single consciousness, each influenced by our local environments, but one all the same.

> *We are extensions of the same single consciousness, each influenced by our local environments, but one all the same.*

Contemplate this. As you are deeply connected to this moment, ask your intuition if this is true. **Ask if you are ready to allow this. This is a big step. Take your time.**

The Big Bang And The One Consciousness (A Thought Experiment)

Sentient consciousness creates everything.

The idea that there is only one consciousness and we are it, can be hard to grasp but a bit of modern Quantum Mechanics and Astrophysics helps us to see how this could be so. In this thought experiment we aggregate various results to reach a profound conclusion.

Laboratory experiments have shown that both photons (massless) and electrons (massed) behave like waves until measured / observed and only then collapse into a particle, and that this physical existence as a particle is temporary, lasting only as long as observed. This "observation" is defined as, and has been shown to be, the concept being generated in the mind of a sentient human being.

Separate experiments on electrons in energy wells show that all matter is energy, existing everywhere all the time (according to a probability density function) until our observation collapses its wave function, forcing it to "choose" a location in which to exist in physical form.

Zeno noted that we observe, periodically, the location of things. Our minds take this series of observations, like snapshots, and string them together into a linear story in order to make sense of it (the arrow of time).

Therefore, sentient consciousness creates everything. **Nothing exists until a sentient consciousness conceives of it.** Everything exists as what we will call potential existence (energy), until a sentient consciousness manifests it (collapses the wave functions) into what we here will call kinetic existence (matter).

So here is the really interesting question: **how and when did the FIRST sentient consciousness come into existence?** The first sentient consciousness could not have come into physical existence (kinetic existence) without first existing as potential existence (energy). Let's approach this logically.

Either:

(1) There was a time post-Big-Bang when NO sentient consciousness existed, or

(2) A sentient consciousness always existed since the Big Bang (and possibly before).

Let's start with the first case. Suppose that there was a time, after the big bang, when this universe had no sentient consciousness (in energy form or otherwise). During this time, no wave forms would collapse from observation and thus everything would exist as energy (waves) everywhere all the time and physical objects would not have come into existence. It would be a universe of 100% potential existence (energy only). There would be nothing to manifest the manifestor or create the creator, and a sentient consciousness itself would never come into existence, much less planets, stars, and people.

You could argue that there are forces we don't understand that could have brought the first sentient consciousness into existence and the fact that there are lots of things we don't understand is certainly true. Another argument is that sentience was a byproduct of evolution here on earth, but in that case, there would have been no sentient being to manifest (collapse wave functions to create) the earth in order for evolution to get started.

Thus, a sentient consciousness always existed, at least since the Big Bang, and maybe before

Therefore, it cannot be true that, at the big bang there was not a sentient consciousness but that later there was. Thus, a sentient consciousness always existed, at least since the Big Bang, and maybe before.

What if the big bang was the BIRTH of a sentient consciousness? What if it is one of many?

What if, in the field of potential existence, consciousnesses springs into being - each a universe birthed by a big bang. This consciousness (if we think in linear terms - which is human to do) is consumed in creative play in a space of potential existence within itself, creating more and more complicated things: particles, forces, stars, planets, plants, creatures, etc.

Every religion in the world has a deity. This deity existed, they say, since the beginning and created everything. But what was there to create with? There was only the deity. Everything was therefore made from that deity, by that deity. This is the one consciousness. Here are some useful analogies... I can take a block of clay and make many different beautiful cups, bowls, plates, and statues, but they are all inherently the one block of clay. In this case, the one consciousness was both the clay and the artist and it created everything from itself. Similarly, a mother uses only one cell from the father to create a child. Her body creates the child from the materials available within herself, and then releases the child into the world. **The child is an extension of the mother, made from the mother and by the mother.** And so as we trace existence all the way back, we see that we (people, places, stars, etc.) are all extensions of the one consciousness, made by the one consciousness, from the material of the one consciousness.

We (people, places, stars, etc.) are all extensions of the one consciousness, made by the one consciousness, from the material of the one consciousness.

This original sentient consciousness is within us - we are all part of the same whole that manifested us and we can also in turn manifest new things.

Similarly, we humans (and other animals, etc) are brought forth into physical existence in a singular ecstatic episode (a mini-big bang at the cellular level upon conception) and are drawn to play. We create things and we create other conscious beings that are drawn to create and play and manifest - and onward it goes.

We humans are part of the larger consciousness. We are physical manifestations of the original consciousness, and we are embedded with that consciousness, and as such can, and desire to, create and play and manifest. **We are everything, everywhere, through all time.** If there is a universal creator - we are part of it, and it is in us and around us... we are the part and whole of it.

We can manifest anything, not because we are special humans or somehow "chosen," but because we ARE the universal consciousness. Any sentient being (any creation that has the consciousness, or any manifestation that the consciousness inhabits) can manifest anything, from the space of potential existence into the space of kinetic existence. That is, from energy to matter.

We create things and we create other things that can create things of their own. We manifest - and not all that creatively, actually. We tend to manifest evolutionarily, at every level: planetary, species, cellular, etc. rather than revolutionarily.

We can manifest anything, not because we are special humans or somehow "chosen," but because we ARE the universal consciousness.

It begs the question, then... Why don't we all know that we are the one consciousness? I think we do know it, but we are conditioned into believing that we are separate from each other and all things. We are conditioned to believe in deities that can create but we are told that they are separate from us. And not knowing (or not having confidence that we inherently know), we buy it all and so separate ourselves from everything. Because you can manifest anything: if you decide that you are separate, so you are.

Because you can manifest anything: if you decide that you are separate, so you are.

What if everything we learn as small children is wrong? We learn:

- I am separate from mom and dad and everyone.

- I am just this body.

- My existence has a boundary which is these parts and not beyond.

- Object permanence - the object is still there, even if I cannot see it.

- There is a larger force or deity in the universe but it has no connection to me.

Maybe it's time to trust our intuition. But if you are not ready to trust your intuition, trust the Physics instead.

Connecting To Your Intellect - Building Skills For Your Purpose

In Stage Eight, you found your purpose, or at least a good idea of what your purpose might be. Now it is time to gather the skills and knowledge you will need to forward your purpose. What skills and knowledge will you need to make the best possible effort towards your purpose? Do you need to learn specific software tools and apps? Do you need another language? Do you need physical skills or abilities? Do you simply need more knowledge about certain subjects? **Write it all down. Even if these skills sound impossible, write them down anyway. Many things are easier than you think. And you are definitely smarter than you think.** For extra inspiration, add in skills and knowledge you will need for anything on your list of things you have always wanted to try, do or experience. It is no coincidence that these things are related to your purpose.

As you list these skills and knowledge, there will be, guaranteed, a voice inside your head that tells you this is crazy, or you aren't smart enough or it will never work. As humans, we all have this negative voice that works to pull us towards mediocrity. Any effort to forward yourself will be met with this negative voice. And the greater the effort, the louder the negative voice. Move forward anyway. Everyone you ever admired had it. Everyone who ever did anything great had it. The key is to tell it to shut up. Quite simply, make it clear that you are not going to listen. The more you dismiss it, and the more you feed your desire to carry out your purpose, the weaker that negative voice gets.

Now, make a plan to get those skills and that knowledge. For large or intimidating skills and learning, break it down into small parts that you can do each day. If you are learning a language, start with one word per day. If you need to read a big stack of books, start with one page or one chapter per day. Learning a new app or software tool? Start with one tutorial video per day. Starting with small efforts gives you momentum and progress that will build naturally. You will quickly have the skills and knowledge you need. Consistent effort is the key.

The greater the effort, the louder the negative voice. Move forward anyway. Consistent effort is the key.

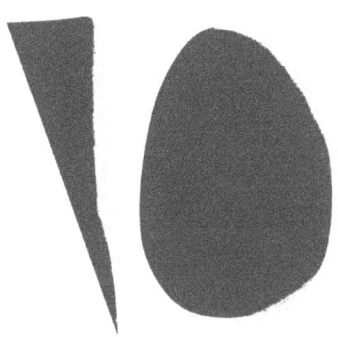

Stage Ten: I Am The ONE Consciousness

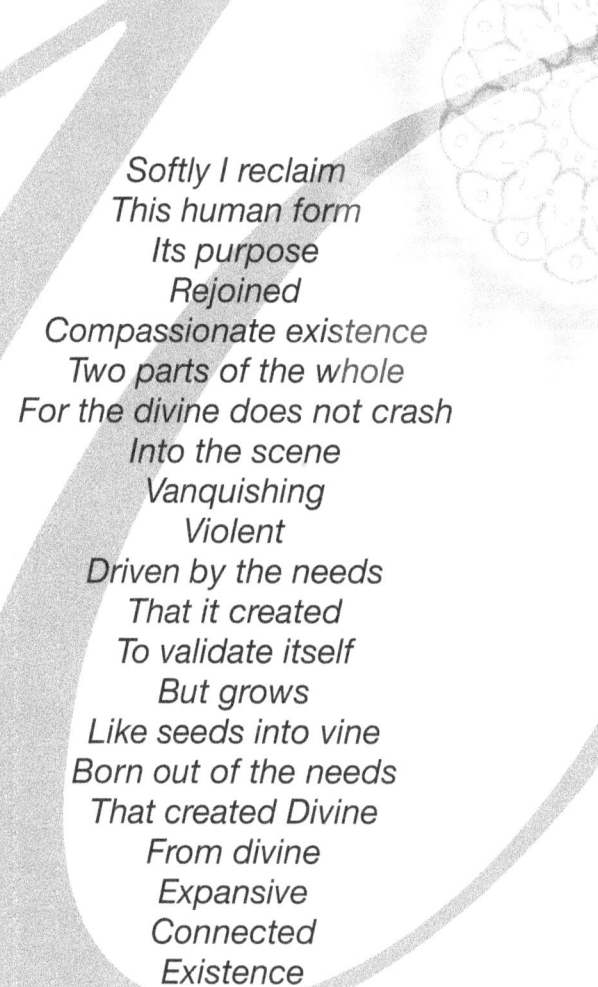

Softly I reclaim
This human form
Its purpose
Rejoined
Compassionate existence
Two parts of the whole
For the divine does not crash
Into the scene
Vanquishing
Violent
Driven by the needs
That it created
To validate itself
But grows
Like seeds into vine
Born out of the needs
That created Divine
From divine
Expansive
Connected
Existence

CHARACTERISTICS

- You realize that there is only one consciousness. You are an extension of that, as is everyone and everything else.
- You trust your intuition and begin to listen to it more often, training it to tell you what you need to know.
- You live in the moment, not worrying about the future or reliving the past.

CHALLENGES

The biggest challenge in this stage is maintaining the feeling of oneness that you have with everyone and everything. If you try to maintain it, it fades away. You have to not try, and just be in the now, feeling it, flowing in the moment. Be cognizant of how easily you can be pulled back around the cycle into other stages.

TASKS

☐ **Connect to higher wisdom.**

☐ **Connect to the oneness and your influence.**

☐ **Recognize the triggers** that take you out of this stage and make efforts to guard your environment accordingly.

Don't forget to:

☐ Stay connected to this moment.

☐ Stay connected to your intuition, the infinite peace/divine and silent observer inside you.

☐ Stay connected to your energy, body, feelings, sexuality, health, money, needs, humanity and truth.

☐ Update your principles and ideology as new experiences shape you.

> ### Resources
>
> - *Biocentrism* by Robert Lanza, MD
> - *The Wim Hof Method* (video series)

Questions To Fuel Your Thinking

- What do you want for your life right now? Why?

- What do you feel compelled to do? Is it compelling or impulse?

- What does the energy inside you feel like? Where in your body do you feel it? How does it feel differently in different parts of your body?

- What are the triggers that pull you back around the cycle?

- What practices, guidelines, and processes can you put in place to safeguard your time in this stage?

Connecting To Higher Wisdom - Beyond Intuition

In Stage Nine, you practiced connecting with your intuition by connecting deeply with each moment. Now that you recognize that there is only one consciousness, and you are an extension or part of that, you have access to a higher level of wisdom and guidance. **In moments when you need, or simply would like divine guidance, it is yours.**

Be still and listen. Ask for guidance. Feel your presence as the one consciousness. Feel the divine nature of that consciousness. Reach out through this infinite existence. Feel the presence of other extensions of that consciousness here to guide you.

Have you ever felt, intuitively, the presence of a long lost family member? Or a dear friend who has left this physical existence? Do they appear to you in dreams? You can feel their presence now if you want to. These people who were connected to us in life often return to help us along. But they are not the only ones. Beings of pure energy or light, whom you have not met before, may also come along to help you.

Be still and listen. Ask for guidance. Feel your presence as the one consciousness.

For some very skilled in this work, you may be able to see them, or feel physical contact from them. If that is not the case, or you do not want that kind of experience, you are not any less connected to them. They are here to help, regardless. They are conduits of divine wisdom and guidance to help you toward your purpose.

The effect of reaching even one person with true connection can change the course of humanity.

If you can learn to hear their guidance speaking through your intuition, you can accelerate towards your purpose and ideal life. **Your guides will make you feel compelled to do what is in your highest interests.** Pursue what you are compelled to do but carefully note why you are compelled (do not pursue activities that come from from a place of ego, fear, or other negative emotions). **As you learn to distinguish compelling from impulse, recognizing higher wisdom becomes easy.**

So welcome your guides. You may find they each specialize in specific kinds of help. Some may focus on preparing you for particular tasks, ensuring your safety, or guarding your purpose. Others may play a more expanded role.

If the idea of guides assigned to you feels humbling, that is a good thing. We are too often taught that we do not matter. We too often feel that we would not be missed. But the divine has a purpose for you and has sent help to make it happen. If that makes you feel important, it should, because you are. **You are the only one who can carry out YOUR unique purpose.** Your purpose may be simple or grandiose, but the effect of reaching even one person with true connection can change the course of humanity. And the whole of creation is looking forward to it.

Connecting To The Oneness And Your Influence

At this point, you recognize your physical body and the one consciousness that is within your body, all people, places and things. **Try this...**

1. Feel the energy inside you.
2. Practice being the energy or being the physical body/mind (alternate back and forth).
3. Feel what it is like to be other people, places and things.
4. Feel what it is like to just be the energy/consciousness separate from the body.

This is a fun exercise that helps you to connect with all sides. You will find that you can control how you choose to exist in this moment. You are always anchored in this physical form, but you can be the energy or the physical.

> *You are always anchored in this physical form, but you can be the energy or the physical.*

With that understanding, it is time to learn how much influence you really have. **As the one consciousness, you have influence worldwide, and across time.** Notice how your thoughts, combined with feeling, change your world. Notice how you can manifest people, places, things, opportunities, and anything else.

> *More connected = more capable.*

You have probably been trying this all along, but you may have noticed that you are more effective now. No, you are not ALL POWERFUL. Your guides will attempt to block anything that takes you away from your purpose. But anything you might request that forwards your purpose, or at least does not take away from it, will be granted now much more quickly.

Why? You have more experience now and your connection is deeper and more complete. You are simply more capable now because you are more connected to yourself, your energy, this moment, others and your life. More connected = more capable.

Understand that do not have control. Control is a form of attachment. **What you have is INFLUENCE.** Your expanding influence can be exciting, frightening and humbling. You might fear that it will go to your head. You might fear that the universe/divine expects too much from you. Good. **You must pass through this phase of fear to reach a balanced command of your influence** that is humble and respects its power. If you have not felt these fears yet, you have not yet realized the full extent of your influence. Give it time.

When you recognize an emotional or ancestral issue that you have trouble clearing on your own, use your influence to request help. Practice optimizing any and every aspect of your life as you like. Enjoy this process. Manifest your ideal life from a place of joy and peace, allowing your influence to grow naturally into its full potential.

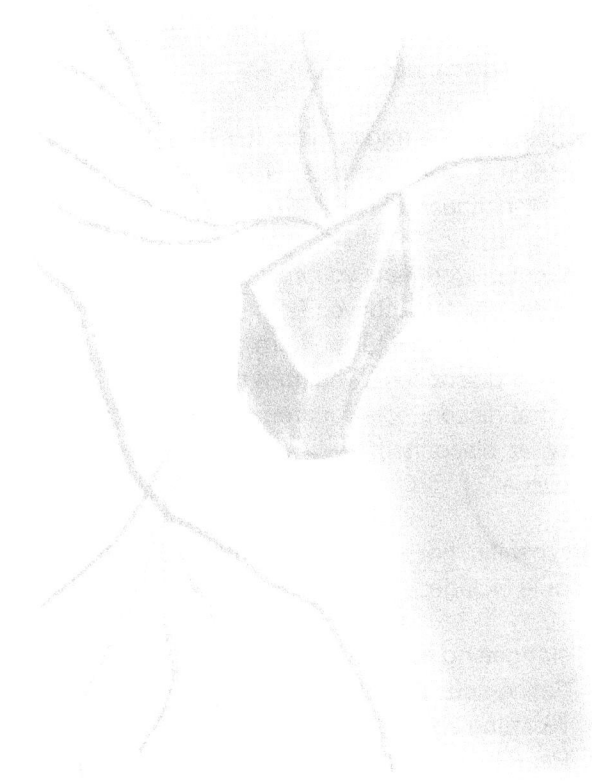

Staying Connected - Recognizing Separation Triggers

Connecting to the oneness and this moment; living in that space, is easier for you to do each time you try. However, you are not immune to life. There will be a steady stream of triggers that will take you out of this stage. **Life happens, and we become disconnected from the oneness, from the moment, from others, from ourselves and from life.** This is a good time to craft an environment that keeps you in these later stages as long as possible, and helps get you back here quickly when you become disconnected.

Connection is a fragile thing. It is easily broken. Take some time now to write down the types of situations that disconnect you...

- What disconnects you from yourself?
- What disconnects you from your energy?
- What disconnects you from others?
- What disconnects you from this moment?
- What disconnects you from life and purpose?
- What disconnects you from the oneness or the divine?

Be specific. For example, common triggers for many people include:

- Not getting enough exercise or movement
- Eating specific foods
- Worrying about specific future problems
- Regretting specific past events
- Reading or watching the news
- Looking at social media
- Watching too much TV
- Negative self talk
- Treating your purpose as unimportant
- Missing your mediation or prayer
- Distractions that come between you and your friends or partner
- Illness or injury
- Elections
- Specific people who seem to pull you back into earlier stages
- Lack of sexual fulfillment or connection
- Work stress
- The daily commute

These are just a few ideas. **Triggers are very individual and your list may look different.**

Craft an environment that keeps you in these later stages as long as possible, and helps get you back here quickly when you become disconnected.

Once you know what causes you to disconnect, you can craft an environment that avoids it as much as possible. For example, you might find ways to make your daily commute a source of connection, instead of disconnection, by calling a loved one or listening to books or podcasts that are fun or give you fuel for your purpose. You might organize your calendar to ensure time for exercise, and quality time connecting with your partner. You might make a rule that phones and devices are not allowed when you gather with friends. One idea is to place all the phones face down on the table and the first person to pick their phone up has to pay the bill. Get creative. **Make connection a priority.**

Ultimately, life WILL take you around the cycle again. BUT, you can, with these safeguards in place, get back to these blissful later stages quickly and stay there longer.

What changes will you make to safeguard your connection?

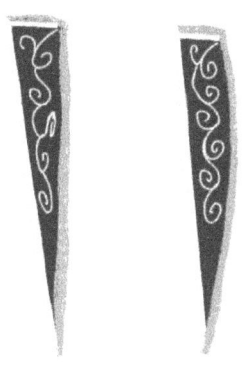

Stage Eleven: I Am The One Consciousness & The Physical Manifestation Simultaneously And There Is No Difference

*And the divine
emerges
quietly
Born unto the scene
That coaxes it forward
Like an orchid
Slowly
Fed on the energy
of allowing
And the light
of letting be
Perfectly imperfect
The divine resolves
into sight
And the shadows
of what came before
Fade away
Imperceptibly
Until
There
Are
None*

Characteristics

- You feel the one consciousness, here in this human body, experiencing what it is like to be human - to ignore your humanity would be to miss out on the experience.
- You are matter and energy at the same time. You can consciously choose to experience the moment as either one, or both.
- There is no difference between the energy and the physical.
- You can consciously influence your reality to actively build an ideal life for yourself and alter it as your ideal evolves.
- You live in purpose, peace and joy.
- You connect deeply with yourself, your loved ones, friends and strangers.
- You exude a peace and joy that make people want to be near you.

Challenges

Maintenance, Maintenance, Maintenance. There is a lot to maintain at this point: your needs, your ideology, your experiences, your sense of connectedness and oneness. Once you have tasted this stage, you may find yourself crafting a life for yourself that will let you spend as much time here as possible. That ideal life will look very different for each of us. As you create space for further (yes, further!) development, you can begin to experiment with actively creating complete connection to yourself, your world, others, etc. Complete connection can help you to return to this stage and stay there as long as possible. In addition to actively creating complete connection, allow your naturally connected state to exist by removing whatever may be covering it up and blocking it. Actively seek complete connection, and simultaneously relax and allow that complete connection to happen.

TASKS

☐ **Connect to your reality.**

☐ Actively and consciously **design and create your ideal life** and your ideal self. Live in your purpose with peace and joy.

☐ **Recognize** when you are cycling through the stages again. Remember that life will take you around the circle many times but YOU are in control of how much time you spend in each stage.

☐ **Ripples in the water** - the strong, consistent signal wins.

☐ **Enjoy your human existence** in all of its most basic aspects as well as its more subtle complexities.

☐ **Seek complete connection** with yourself, with others, with this moment, your life at large, your money, your purpose, etc.

Don't forget to:

☐ Stay connected to this moment.

☐ Stay connected to your intuition, the infinite peace/divine and silent observer inside you.

☐ Stay connected to your energy, body, feelings, sexuality, health, money, needs, humanity and truth in this moment.

☐ Update your principles and ideology as new experiences shape you.

Resources

- This book! - *Purna Asatti*
- *On Life And Being Human* Podcast by Kathryn Colleen (send in your questions).

Questions To Fuel Your Thinking

- What daily and/or weekly practices can you put in place to process experiences, understand your changing needs and meet them, understand your evolving ideologies and maintain perspective?

- What regular practices can you put in place to create and maintain complete connection to yourself? To others? To this moment? To this world? To the oneness?

- Can you craft an efficient and effective daily routine that helps you spend the maximum time possible in this stage? What would that look like?

Connecting To Your Reality - $E = mc^2$

Einstein was right. Energy IS matter. Literally. There is no difference. It is a fact of Physics that most of us ignore; even the Physicists. At this point, you have some experience connecting to moments as the energy or as the physical form. **Now it is time to dissolve any separation between them.**

Try the following...

Be here in this moment, as you have before.

Connect to the energy in this space.

Connect to the physical objects in this space.

Connect to the people.

Now connect to the energy again.

This time, as you focus on existing as the energy, think about how sparse these physical objects are.

According to Jefferson Labs, "A hydrogen atom is about 99.9999999999996% empty space." All the other atoms are similar with small variations. And what is in that space? Nothing but the energy binding it all together. So that table or chair you are looking at is not at all solid. Can you feel the energy go right through that object? Can you see it almost start to dissolve in front of you as you focus on its energy instead of its physical existence?

Look at the room around you now. Can you focus on the energy and see it? **When doing this exercise effectively, you will see a kind of hazy blur within the room.** People skilled in energy work or mediation might even witness the dissolution of objects and people. But for most of us, it is a feeling that things are about to break apart and dissolve into the energy.

It can be a little intimidating and you might find yourself holding back intentionally as the human mind fears losing itself. Nothing bad will happen if you relax into this and allow the energy to dissolve the physical. **You are not changing your reality, you are changing your perception of reality.**

This is a similar experience to psychedelic compounds, but we have arrived here without that.

Can you see it almost start to dissolve in front of you as you focus on its energy instead of its physical existence?

If you find you could use some help reaching this state, psychedelic compounds will certainly do the trick, but are not necessary. Methods such as "Wim Hof Breathing" and focused mediation will give you an equivalent altered state.

This state of mind is an "altered consciousness" and very hard to maintain even for the most practiced person. When you feel yourself falling out of it, consciously drop back to Stage Ten, feeling yourself as both the energy and the physical manifestation.

When you feel yourself falling out of it, consciously drop back to Stage Ten.

You may find that this stage of complete oneness is a quick vacation each day, rather than a more permanent state. There is a risk of coming out of this stage and rolling right into Stage Three by feeling disappointment at losing it, or engaging in negative self talk, expectations, or attachment to the state of complete oneness. It is so blissful that it can become somewhat addictive. Instead of letting attachment send you around the cycle again, just drop back into Stage Ten, stay there for a few minutes to solidify it and go about your day in Stage Ten. That way, you can return to Stage Eleven easily enough without losing your beautiful state.

Maintaining It All

How can you stay in this beautiful place as long as possible? There is an art and a science to maintaining later stages...

First, actively and consciously design and create your ideal life and your ideal self. Be careful to understand WHY you want what you want. Create from a place of positive emotion and positive intent. Be careful what you wish for AND why you wish for it. **And do it CONSISTENTLY**.

Lots of people are, at any moment, sending out signals to manifest what they want. The interaction of those signals is like the ripples made by tossing several stones into a pond. If I drop a larger stone into the pond, it makes a big strong wave that affects a larger area. If I drop a small stone, it makes a smaller wave, affecting a smaller area. However, if you drop a large stone only once, and I drop one small stone after another, my smaller waves will eventually dominate your space.

Actively and consciously design and create your ideal life and your ideal self.

The lesson is that it's not just about sending a strong signal, it's about sending a strong signal every day. If you take a break from sending your signal, you open the opportunity for competing signals to affect your life. You allow someone else to influence your world. Sometimes that is a good thing and sometimes that may not be healthy for you.

The solution is, at first, to define every aspect of what you want your world to be, and then send out that signal daily. (As an important warning, **be sure to focus on what you DO want** and not on what you do not want. Review the guidelines for manifesting for other important caveats).

Try to cover these areas...

- Spiritual
- Emotional
- Intellectual
- Physical (overall health, metabolic, strength, speed, autophagy, flexibility, etc)
- Social (types of social interactions, energy, etc)
- Financial (income, outgo, etc)
- Lifestyle
- Locations
- Opportunities
- Things
- Etc

In other words, define your self and your life, or someone else will define it for you. Think on it and feel it every day to not only bring about the changes that you want but to maintain the beautiful life that you have built.

And then what? Then the laundry and the dishes still need to be done, and the house must still be repaired. Enjoy your human existence in all of its most basic aspects as well as its more subtle complexities. Integrate these aspects into your coherent whole.

As your connections become more integrated, you will naturally move to defining and manifesting your life in more general but protective terms. For example, you might manifest a life that is protected, exciting, peaceful, joyous and forwards your purpose. Such a definition prevents negative influences, but leaves the details for the divine. Such a life is full of surprises and can be even more amazing than you could have imagined. **It is all up to you!**

Seeking Complete Connection

As you enjoy life in the later stages, one way to stay there significantly longer is to actively seek complete connection with yourself, with others, with this moment, your life at large, your money, your purpose, etc. **As you craft a routine that helps to keep you in later stages, include activities that deepen your connections**: exercise, mediation or prayer time, time to think, time to connect with your partner, and whatever else works best for you.

Remember that you still have needs, you still have an ideology (based on principles at this point) and you still have a self (all necessary to get through the day) - attend to them, evolve them, but do not ignore them and do not become attached to them.

Remember that life will take you around the circle many times but YOU are in control of how much time you spend in each stage. Use what you have learned here and refer back to this writing to...

(1) Recognize when you are cycling through the stages again,

(2) Take care of any new or leftover tasks from those earlier stages and

(3) Bring yourself back to the later stages as efficiently as possible.

With time and practice, you will find yourself spending more and more time in blissful later stages and less and less time in earlier stages. That is, you will spend more and more time feeling joy, peace, love, adventure or other positive emotions of your choosing and less and less time with the negative ones. **Life becomes an increasing spiral of amazing.**

This is both a process and a life long practice.

So here is to your amazing life and your complete connection.

Purna Asatti.

This is both a process and a life long practice.

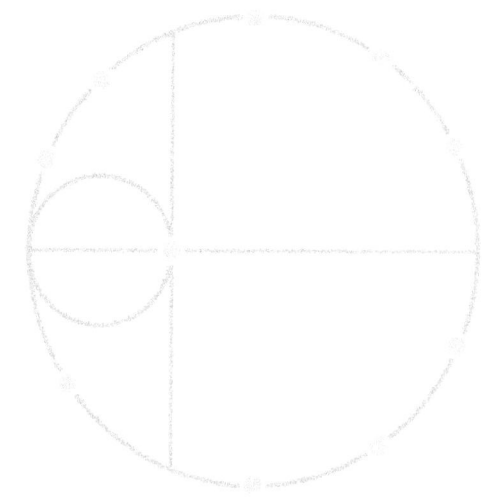

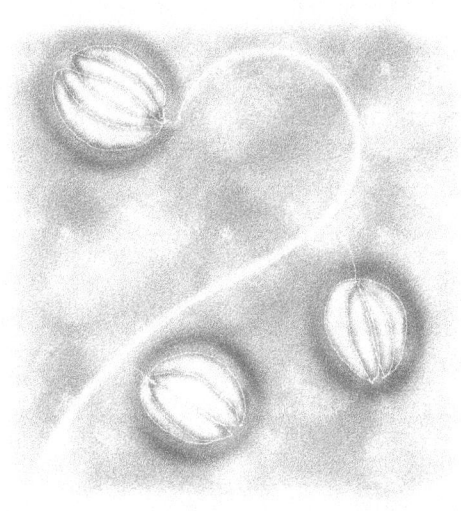

Accelerating Your Development

Mentors, Teachers, Guides And Coaches

When doing anything new, it helps to have a mentor. Mentors, teachers, guides and coaches have been a critical and transformative part of my journey. Some were dear friends who shepherded me through dark times, some were professional guides that I met regularly and some were teachers who shared their knowledge and experience to help me gain specific skills. Many of them were gurus in my eyes. It was an ideal combination that I am sure I would have been lost without. **Their contribution cannot be overstated and I am forever grateful.**

Step one is to recognize when a credible mentor comes into your awareness. While the vast majority of available mentors, teachers, guides and coaches are credible and capable, there are a few who are outright charlatans. As always, there are those in stages three or five who would use you for their own needs or to forward their own agenda. Fortunately, they are easy to recognize.

Ask yourself the following questions:

When they speak, do they refer to themselves more than they refer to you or others? Do they speak of their "needs"? They are in Stage Three and likely to use you to fulfill their own needs, with no regard to yours.

Do they focus on right and wrong, us versus them, and the enemy? Do they talk about the cause and how vital you are? Do they ask you to prove your loyalty? They are in Stage Five and likely to use your time, effort and money to forward their own agenda, but will be the first person to turn on you.

Look for mentors that are further along in their own personal development.

Find the right match for your personality, goals and learning style.

Overall, if they ask you to give up all your possessions, move into their ashram, or otherwise want you to do a lot for them while they do nothing for you, RUN.

Look for mentors that are further along in their own personal development. People who spend a lot of time in later stages speak of compassion, oneness, peace, joy, and your dreams. They focus on what you want to accomplish and they light up when you make a breakthrough. They celebrate your progress and lift you up. **They see your potential and stop at nothing until you see it too.**

Once you feel that a mentor is credible, the next step is to make sure they are a good match for you, specifically. For some subjects, you may prefer a masculine or feminine mentor. For other subjects, you might consider someone older or younger.

While experience obviously matters, effectiveness is the most important. Ultimately, you want to learn, or progress, or gain new perspective.

Do you like a high energy approach or something more calm and peaceful? Do you need accountability, motivation, or just some ideas of what to try? Do you like to learn in a group, or is one-on-one best?

Do you need someone who specializes in one particular thing like energy work, and another who specializes in personal development? Or would you respond better to someone who is more all-in-one, with lots of different tools available? For example, some massage therapists are also skilled in energy work and personal guidance.

You will find that **a good teacher or guide, as you progress, is learning from you even as you are learning from them.** It is an exchange that accelerates your development and enriches both of you.

The ultimate dream team of mentors for you may be a combination of specialists and multi-talented advisors. What do you need to work on? What skills or perspectives do you need? Ask your river for the mentors you need. When they appear, don't let the opportunity get away.

You might find mentors among your friends, your family, coworkers, or within your professional network. Other mentors might come to you in your reading, at local events or in web searches. Teachers of all kinds are all around you.

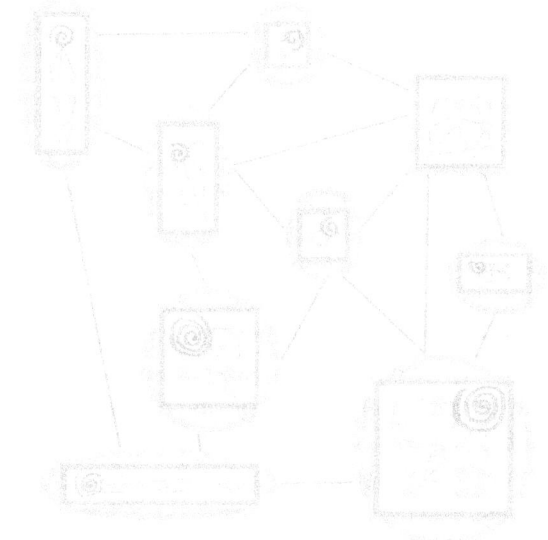

Reiki And The Role Of Energy Work

I have experimented with a large number of methods for self development. If it exists, I have probably tried it. **Reiki, a form of energy work, is the single most effective method of accelerating your development that I have ever seen.** The difference is months instead of years. Literally, a "10X" improvement. I was so impressed with Reiki and what it did for me, that I stopped at nothing to achieve the rank of Reiki Master Teacher; just because I had to know how it works and everything about it.

When you are sick, worried, angry, or fearful, you feel exhausted. You lack energy, because these emotions and illnesses drain your energy, literally. You are out of balance.

The experience was nothing short of profoundly healing and transformational. Once I learned the full range of what it was capable of, I started using it here and there, as appropriate, with my students. The results were more than impressive. **I have watched students go from stuck in stage five to physically experiencing their spirit guides and finding true self mastery in as little as six months.** It is so effective that I often have to encourage students to slow down a bit. Fast progress can be overwhelming.

Reiki, as we know it today, is a form of energy healing originating in Japan in the early 1900s. It was brought to the west in the 1930s. Today, there are Reiki programs at some hospitals for infants and adults alike. There are Reiki programs at Hospice organizations for end of life. There are Reiki practitioners who focus on emotional issues, or animals, and everything between.

So what is it, exactly? Reiki is the life force energy in everything you see. When you are sick, worried, angry, or fearful, you feel exhausted. You lack energy, because these emotions and illnesses drain your energy, literally. You are out of balance. But when you are healthy, joyous, at peace or purposeful, you feel full of energy, because you are. The more of this energy that you have in you, the more balanced and healthy you feel. And balance is what it's all about.

Reiki is good at bringing balance to your body, emotions, intellect, energy, and mind. For example, if you are starting to get a cold, or if you have a tummy ache, Reiki can help you heal yourself. If you are stressed out and worried or spun up from work, Reiki can you calm yourself down. Balance looks like health and peace and joy. And Reiki helps you bring yourself into balance.

The Reiki practitioner is a conduit for the energy.

I say that it helps YOU to do it, because you are precisely the one doing it. The Reiki practitioner is a conduit for the energy. They channel the energy and concentrate it in their hands. When they place their hands on your head, shoulders, feet or various chakra points, your energy field and body respond by drawing in as much energy as you may need. It is your being that decides how much energy to pull in and how to use it to create balance.

In my own experimentation, I have found that Reiki is great for acute physical issues and emotional/mental issues. It is great for calming children (especially special needs children), babies, veterans, and just stressed out working spouses. It cannot, however, save you from your food allergies, or from gaining weight when you eat badly, or from your own negative intentions. It cannot save you from what you do not want to be saved from. And it is not a substitute for medical treatment. It IS, however a very nice addition to your medical team and an amazingly effective addition to your personal development efforts, as well as a nice addition to family life.

The more advanced the practitioner, the more effective and profound the experience, and the faster you will progress.

When trying Reiki for the first time, make sure that you have a hands-on treatment and not a hands-off treatment. Some practitioners send Reiki while keeping their hands anywhere from several inches to several feet away from the patient. If this is your first Reiki treatment, you may not feel it. With a hands-on treatment, the practitioner lays their hands lightly on the patient for several minutes in each spot. The difference that touch makes is vital to your experience.

You do not have to believe in it for it to work, just like you do not have to believe that if you drop an object, it will hit the ground. It just works.

When choosing a practitioner, look for a fully credentialed practitioner, and a Reiki Master Teacher, if possible. **A good practitioner will not be offended if you ask for a copy if their certificate.** Why seek a master? With each level of learning, the Reiki practitioners receive "attunements" and "ignitions" which expand the amount of energy they are capable of delivering. There are four levels: Level One, Level Two, Advanced (sometimes called master practitioner), and Master Teacher. While you will get significant benefit, in my opinion, from practitioners at any of these levels, the more advanced the practitioner, the more effective and profound the experience, and the faster you will progress.

You might even decide to learn Reiki for yourself. Some people choose to learn Level One just to have the benefit of giving Reiki to themselves and their immediate family. Some prefer not to learn Reiki, because it would spoil the air of magic when receiving it. The right answer is to just try it once and see what you think. If your intuition says to do more, then do more. **Whatever you are called to is the right answer.**

I find myself now with the power to help people find peace nearly instantly, and to help them accelerate their personal journeys. It is a power that I cannot scientifically explain. It is nice to have something that you cannot explain but yet the results are undeniable. You do not have to believe in it for it to work, just like you do not have to believe that if you drop an object, it will hit the ground. It just works. This bit of wonder in the world is cause for us all to pause and question whether we really understand anything at all. The world is so much more amazing and wondrous than we realize. Trapped in our bubbles of everyday life and schedules, we can lose sight of what is important. Reiki can bring us back to it.

Meanwhile, I credit Reiki for accelerating my students' evolution through the stages and for helping me spend more and more time in later stages 10 and 11. This is truly a pragmatic and yet deeply soul-stirring technique. The fact that it employs connection (as gentle touch or virtual connection) is likely a large part of why it works so well.

I encourage you to find a practitioner and experiment with Reiki for yourself. Some massage therapists can incorporate Reiki into a session for multi-dimensional relaxation. It is well worth a try.

Questions, Answers And Additional Resources

Do you have questions about what you have read here? Go to the Community Page at <u>KathrynColleen.com</u> and use the form to send in your questions. Kathryn will answer you back as quickly as possible and may include your question on the podcast or blog.

Also at <u>KathrynColleen.com</u>, you will find:

- The music album, Purna Asatti, that accompanies this book

- The podcast where many of your questions may be answered.

- Other books, albums, essays and art by Kathryn Colleen.

- And more!

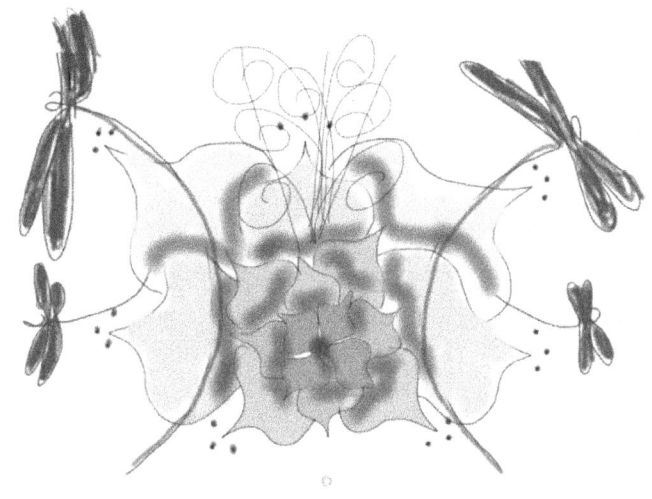

Big List Of Great Questions

When all the hard work of your journey is largely over, sometimes it is fun to pick a random question and think. What follows is a big random list of great questions to choose from. Enjoy!

When was the last time you….

- felt safe?

- fest at peace?

- felt alive?

- felt purposeful?

- said something nice to yourself?

- said something critical to yourself?

- learned something new about yourself?

- learned something new about the world?

- did something for yourself?

- did something for someone else?

Are you on a path towards…

- a better you?

- a life that makes you feel _____ ?

What do you want? (people, places, things, experiences, feelings, opportunities, etc)

- Why do you want this?

- What is the underlying emotion behind your reasons?

What kind of person do you want to be…

- physically?

- mentally?

- emotionally?

- spiritually?

If this were your last day/week/month/year/5 years/etc, how would you spend it?

What 20% of the people/places/things/activities cause 80% of your joy/peace/frustration/sadness/etc?

If you could design your perfect day-to-day life, what would it look like? (after the beach and the travel wears off)

What would you do differently if you did not care what people thought?

Look back over your past major decisions… what drove them? What emotion was at the heart of it? How did they turn out?

How can you be a better friend to yourself?

If you were your own best friend, what frank conversation would you have with yourself?

How do you speak to yourself?

What kind of friend do you need to be for yourself? (kind, blunt, frank, comforting, etc)

What advice would you give your younger self? Are you following that now?

What advice would your older self give you right now?

What can you do today that your future self will thank you for? Or to make it easier on your future self? To make your future self say, "I am so glad that I…."

What stresses you out or makes you uncomfortable? Why? Why? Why? Why? Why?

What do you keep putting off? Why?

What are your afraid of? Why? How can you confront that fear?

If you did ONE thing today to better yourself or your life, or to move towards your heart's calling, what would it be? (Pick something that takes 15 minutes to 1 hour to do.)

Who or what is standing in your way?

What limiting beliefs do you have from childhood and later?

What freeing beliefs do you have that you can nurture?

What freeing beliefs do you need to program into your mind?

Who inspires you and why?

What are you holding on to that you need to let go of?

Who do you need to forgive? Can you see their humanity and pain hiding within them? Can you see their truth?

How can you be authentically you in a way that brings real value to those around you?

What habits do you need to break?

What habits do you need to start?

What small steps can you make towards breaking or starting those habits?

What aspects of you life are out of line with who you really are?

Who are you really?

What are your needs? (physical, mental, emotional, spiritual, etc)

What are your ideologies? (religious, political, social, moral, etc - your values or principles or beliefs)

What core aspects of your personality have NEVER changed since you were very small?

What has your gut been telling you?

Are you listening?

What have you been lying to yourself about?

What is the truth? (painful or otherwise)

Who can you trust to talk to about this?

How do you feel when you are alone?

What reveals your joy?

If you could live anywhere in the world, where would you live?

What is your purpose?

- What are you uniquely good at?

- What did you want to be when you were 5, 15, 25, 35, ….? Why?

- What do your friends say is the reason they like to have you around? How do you make them FEEL?

- What have you always done, when no one is watching, without being paid, what is it that you MUST do?

- How can you help others?

- What then is your mission here in this life?

What achievements are you most proud of?

What do you wish you had the nerve to do?

What are you grateful for?

What is important to you right now?

Break down how you are spending your time... does your day reflect these priorities?

- How do you spend your hours?

- Is that getting you where you want to be?

- How much of your day do you spend going over the past or worrying about the future? (note: planning and taking action toward the future is not worrying.)

What life rules or philosophy could you write down to guide yourself to have better perspective and/or make better decisions?

Who can mentor you?

Where can you find mentors? (career, spiritual, personal, etc)

What worries you most about the future?

- How can you accept, prepare for and/or mitigate that?

- Can you make it irrelevant?

To what extent have you actually controlled the course of your life to to today?

- What do you wish you had done differently?

- What were your biggest mistakes?

- How can you avoid making those mistakes again?

- What do you need to do now to admit to and resolve the mistakes that are still affecting your life?

Can you return to a point when you were truly yourself on your own path and pick up where you left off?

What experiences shaped you (good and bad)? Can you thank them for shaping you and see that these experiences are not you?

What needs do others have?

- Can you help?

- How would it feel to be them?

- How would it feel to help?

Do you see how others might grow up with or develop a different ideology from you?

Say your name to yourself, in your head… who said that? Who heard that? How can you speak without speaking and hear what makes no sound?

If you are not this body… what are you?

If you are not this mind… what are you?

What if you did the opposite… the opposite of what others have done? The opposite of what everyone thinks is the normal way or the right way?

Who are you trying to be like? Why is it not you?

What would you do differently or the same to be more like YOU?

What do you believe that most people would think is crazy?

What is the difference between surviving, existing, and living?

What would you most like to change about the world?

What does it mean to be human?

If you look into the heart of your enemy… what would you find? How did it get there?

Which of society's rules are wrong?

What is "peace" to you?

What is comforting to you?

What experiences do you want to have?

- How do you have to grow to have those experiences? (skills, etc)
- How can you give back to the world when you are that person?

What is your greatest challenge?

What are you settling for? (There is a difference between accepting your current reality and settling.)

What do you have trouble seeing clearly in your mind?

What 3-5 questions do you wish you had the answers to?

Have you ever made mistakes?

What are you ashamed of?

Have you hurt people in the past?

Can you forgive your humanity?

Where is your money going?

- Where should it be going?

- What could you do if you had no debt payments?

Looking back, how far have you come?

How have you sabotaged yourself?

- Do you have the self control to stop?

- What can you do to support yourself in stopping these behaviors?

What is your "tell" that you are swimming in your baggage? (crying, yelling, etc)

What story can you tell that includes, "… and something in me said…" and it changed your life or saved it? Who was speaking to you?

Notes and Revelations

www.ingramcontent.com/pod-product-compliance
Lightning Source LLC
Chambersburg PA
CBHW062138160426
43191CB00014B/2314